Communications
in Computer and Information Science   1995

Rationale

The CCIS series is devoted to the publication of proceedings of computer science conferences. Its aim is to efficiently disseminate original research results in informatics in printed and electronic form. While the focus is on publication of peer-reviewed full papers presenting mature work, inclusion of reviewed short papers reporting on work in progress is welcome, too. Besides globally relevant meetings with internationally representative program committees guaranteeing a strict peer-reviewing and paper selection process, conferences run by societies or of high regional or national relevance are also considered for publication.

Topics

The topical scope of CCIS spans the entire spectrum of informatics ranging from foundational topics in the theory of computing to information and communications science and technology and a broad variety of interdisciplinary application fields.

Information for Volume Editors and Authors

Publication in CCIS is free of charge. No royalties are paid, however, we offer registered conference participants temporary free access to the online version of the conference proceedings on SpringerLink (http://link.springer.com) by means of an http referrer from the conference website and/or a number of complimentary printed copies, as specified in the official acceptance email of the event.

CCIS proceedings can be published in time for distribution at conferences or as postproceedings, and delivered in the form of printed books and/or electronically as USBs and/or e-content licenses for accessing proceedings at SpringerLink. Furthermore, CCIS proceedings are included in the CCIS electronic book series hosted in the SpringerLink digital library at http://link.springer.com/bookseries/7899. Conferences publishing in CCIS are allowed to use Online Conference Service (OCS) for managing the whole proceedings lifecycle (from submission and reviewing to preparing for publication) free of charge.

Publication process

The language of publication is exclusively English. Authors publishing in CCIS have to sign the Springer CCIS copyright transfer form, however, they are free to use their material published in CCIS for substantially changed, more elaborate subsequent publications elsewhere. For the preparation of the camera-ready papers/files, authors have to strictly adhere to the Springer CCIS Authors' Instructions and are strongly encouraged to use the CCIS LaTeX style files or templates.

Abstracting/Indexing

CCIS is abstracted/indexed in DBLP, Google Scholar, EI-Compendex, Mathematical Reviews, SCImago, Scopus. CCIS volumes are also submitted for the inclusion in ISI Proceedings.

How to start

To start the evaluation of your proposal for inclusion in the CCIS series, please send an e-mail to ccis@springer.com.

Damayanthi Herath · Susumu Date ·
Upul Jayasinghe · Vijaykrishnan Narayanan ·
Roshan Ragel · Jilong Wang

Editors

Asia Pacific Advanced Network

56th International Conference, APANConf 2023
Colombo, Sri Lanka, August 24–25, 2023
Revised Selected Papers

 Springer

Editors
Damayanthi Herath ⓘ
University of Peradeniya
Peradeniya, Sri Lanka

Susumu Date ⓘ
Osaka University
Suita, Osaka, Japan

Upul Jayasinghe ⓘ
University of Peradeniya
Peradeniya, Sri Lanka

Vijaykrishnan Narayanan ⓘ
Pennsylvania State University
University Park, PA, USA

Roshan Ragel ⓘ
University of Peradeniya
Peradeniya, Sri Lanka

Jilong Wang
Tsinghua University
Beijing, China

ISSN 1865-0929   ISSN 1865-0937 (electronic)
Communications in Computer and Information Science
ISBN 978-3-031-51134-9   ISBN 978-3-031-51135-6 (eBook)
https://doi.org/10.1007/978-3-031-51135-6

This Springer imprint is published by the registered company Springer Nature Switzerland AG
The registered company address is: Gewerbestrasse 11, 6330 Cham, Switzerland

Paper in this product is recyclable.

Preface

We are delighted to bring you the proceedings of the Asia Pacific Advanced Network (APAN)56 Conference: APAN56Conf, which is the inaugural APAN conference.

APAN is a key driver in promoting and facilitating network-enabled research and education activities. These include research collaboration, knowledge discovery and sharing, telehealth, and natural disaster mitigation. The members of APAN had their 56th meeting from 21st–25th of August 2023 at Galle Face Hotel, Colombo, Sri Lanka.

These proceedings contain the work presented at the APAN56Conf that happened parallel to the mentioned event on the 24th and 25th of August 2023. The call for papers and participation was shared globally. There were 37 manuscripts submitted for review. Through a double-blind review involving 3 reviews per manuscript on average, 10 full papers and one short paper were accepted for publication. The conference had a lineup of two keynotes followed by 15 presentations of novel and original work under the theme Artificial Intelligence and High Performance Computing (AI and HPC): Better Together, under 3 tracks: Artificial Intelligence and Machine Learning, Accelerated Computing and Distributed Systems, and Communications and Networking. The APAN56Conf was preceded by a Datathon event that happened on the 22nd and 23rd of August. The conference included a closing plenary on the 25th of August on Rebuilding Sri Lanka through Agriculture, Innovation, and Technology.

The APAN56Conf was organized by Lanka Education and Research Network (on behalf of APAN Ltd) in collaboration with the University of Peradeniya, Sri Lanka. We would like to extend our gratitude to Asitha Bandaranayake, Consultant (Chief Technical Officer) of LEARN, who spearheaded the APAN56 meeting, for his continuous support and guidance. We are also grateful to the Springer CCIS editorial team for their invaluable support. To the best of our knowledge, this is the first international conference in Sri Lanka to publish in Springer's Communications in Computer and Information Science series. We extend our sincere gratitude and appreciation to all the authors and reviewers who contributed to the APAN56Conf proceedings intended to present and broaden novel work in AI and HPC: Better Together.

November 2023

Damayanthi Herath
Susumu Date
Upul Jayasinghe
Vijaykrishnan Narayanan
Roshan Ragel
Jilong Wang

Organization

General Chair

Damayanthi Herath   University of Peradeniya, Sri Lanka

Program Committee Chairs

Susumu Date	Osaka University, Japan
Upul Jayasinghe	University of Peradeniya, Sri Lanka
Vijaykrishnan Narayanan	Pennsylvania State University, USA
Roshan G. Ragel	University of Peradeniya, Sri Lanka
Jilong Wang	Tsinghua University, China

Program Committee

Namal Karunarathne	University of Peradeniya, Sri Lanka
Sanka Rasnayake	National University of Singapore, Singapore
Ranga Rodrigo	University of Moratuwa, Sri Lanka

Additional Reviewers

Sachith P. Abeysundara
Nadeesha Adhikari
Janaka Alawatugoda
Thilini Bandara
Rasika Dayarathna
Erunika Dayaratna
Sampath Deegalla
Mahasen B. Dehideniya
Vipula Dissanayake
Dhammika Elkaduwa
Dileepa Fernando
Sachini Herath
Nuwan Janaka
Kumara Kahatapitiya
Titus Kumara Jayarathna

Ruwan D. Nawarathna
Isuru Nawinne
Kamalaruban Parameswaran
Sampath K. Perera
Ruba Prakhash
Jathushan Rajasegaran
Sameera Ramasinghe
Kanchana Ranasinghe
Ranga Rodrigo
Sanjay Saha
Kamalanath Samarakoon
Chamara Sandeepa
Damith Senanayake
Upul Senanayake
Ridwan Shariffdeen

Amila Silva
Shamane Siriwardhana
Ajanthan Thalaiyasingam
Dumindu Tissera
Hakim Usoof

Rajith Vidanaarachchi
Thumeera Wanasinghe Arachchige
Mahanama Wickramasinghe
Dhananjaya Wijerathne
Akshika Wijesundara

Contents

Three-Dimensional Wireless Indoor Localization with Machine Learning Algorithms for Location-Based IoT Applications

M. W. P. Maduranga[1]([⊠]) [iD], H. K. I. S. Lakmal[2] [iD], and L. P. Kalansooriya[1] [iD]

[1] Faculty of Computing, General Sir John Kotelawal Defence University, Ratmalana, Sri Lanka
pasanwellalage@kdu.ac.lk
[2] Department of Mechatronic and Industry Engineering, NSBM Green University Town, Homagama, Sri Lanka

Abstract. This paper presents a novel Machine Learning (ML)-based approach for radio signal-based indoor localizations. In modern location-based Internet of Things (IoT) applications, it is necessary to sense the location of an object within indoor environments. The traditional probabilistic and deterministic algorithms proposed in the literature have several drawbacks. In this work, we propose a localization framework using ML and Received Signal Strength Indication (RSSI) values. During the experiment, we utilized a publicly available UJIIndoorLoc localization dataset containing RSSI values received from known indoor locations. We trained ML algorithms, including Local Gaussian Regression, K-nearest neighbor, Decision Tree Classifier, XGBoost, LightGBM, Support Vector Classifier, and Gaussian Naive Bayes, to predict the location by feeding RSSI values received from the devices at known locations. The experimental results show that XGBoost provides 99% accuracy in terms of localization.

Keywords: Indoor Localization · Deep Learning · Location-based Internet of Things Applications · Smart Cities

1 Introduction

With the advancement of Industry 4.0, Internet of Things (IoT)-based applications have gained widespread popularity. Among these applications, indoor location-based services (LBSs) play a crucial role in IoT implementations [1–3]. These services find applications in asset tracking, monitoring older people in homes, localizing mobile robots, tracking students on smart campuses, monitoring people in shopping malls, and implementing indoor positioning systems (IPS) that leverage geographical location information [4–7]. Various ranging technologies such as Time Difference of Arrival (TDoA), Time of Arrival (ToA), Angle of Arrival (AoA), Received Signal Strength Indicator (RSSI), and Channel State Information (CSI) have been proposed for typical IPS [8]. Each of these technologies has its own advantages and disadvantages; for instance, RSSI requires a simplified hardware setup and accurate signal measurements, while AoA necessitates a complex hardware setup with antenna arrays.

D. Herath et al. (Eds.): APANConf 2023, CCIS 1995, pp. 1–12, 2024.
https://doi.org/10.1007/978-3-031-51135-6_1

To estimate the location in IPS, several algorithms have been proposed, including trilateration, triangulation, and multilateration, which offer decent accuracy [9–11]. The Kalman-filter-based approach provides high accuracy but is impractical for deployment on real-edge devices. More recently, Machine Learning (ML) and Deep Learning (DL) approaches have been applied to IPS design, offering high accuracy, and enabling implementation using cloud-based architectures [12, 13]. Supervised regressors, such as Support Vector Regression (SVR), Random Forest Regressor (RFR), and Decision Tree Regressor (DTR), have been successful in IPS [14–23, 24, 25], and their accuracy is measured using Root Mean Squared Error (RMSE) and coefficient determinant values [15]. Moreover, supervised classifier-based approaches have been developed, utilizing algorithms like Support Vector Machine (SVM), Naïve Bayes, K-nearest neighbor, and Decision Tree classifiers [16]. Evaluation of system performance involves metrics such as accuracy, sensitivity, confusion matrix, and F1-Score. Moreover, ensemble learning-based techniques have been explored to further enhance IPS performance.

DL-based IPS has gained popularity due to its robustness [17–19]. Deep neural networks have the ability to automatically learn features, including various RSSI values received from anchor nodes, mapping inputs to outputs with a higher level of abstraction. Different types of deep neural networks, such as Feed Forward Neural Networks (FFNN), Randomize Neural Networks (RandNN), and Generalized Regression Neural Networks (GRNN), exist, each with its own strengths and weaknesses.

Several studies have proposed location estimation techniques based on artificial neural networks, demonstrating accurate indoor positioning results at a reasonable cost [31]. DL-based IPS has also been applied to localize high-speed moving objects, outperforming traditional methods like the modified Kalman approach [19]. Furthermore, DL has been utilized for localization using over-water electromagnetic signals, showing promising results with meticulous data pre-processing and network training [20]. A proposed approach called DeFLoc combines Deep Learning with FM fingerprint maps, utilizing FM signals for accurate and practical indoor vehicle localization [21].

Although ML-based methods have shown good accuracy in estimation compared to classical localization algorithms, it's important to note that RSSI is highly fluctuating and requires the application of strong filtering techniques and linearization methods on the RSSI dataset before training ML models [21].

Contributions are made on the.

1. Investigate supervised learning techniques for 3D indoor localization
2. Compared different algorithms and analysis the performances.

2   Materials and Methods

2.1   Wireless Indoor Localization Fundamentals

Indoor localization is an important technology that enables the tracking and monitoring of people or objects within buildings where GPS and other satellite technologies may not work or provide accurate results. Wireless sensor networks are one of the most feasible and economical options for indoor positioning and tracking. They can use various techniques such as triangulation, proximity sensing, signal strength measurement, and time of flight to estimate the position of objects or people. The collected location data can then be used for various IoT applications, including tracking animal behavior, air quality monitoring, inventory control, intrusion detection, traffic monitoring, and smart city initiatives. Overall, indoor localization plays a vital role in enabling new applications and improving existing ones by providing accurate and real-time location information.

As shown in Fig. 1, an indoor localization system may consist of multiple anchor nodes and the target node. Where the target node is continuously transmitting its RSSI values to the three anchor nodes simultaneously. The correlation of RSSI values and the distance between the target node and the anchor nodes is expressed below.

$$RSSI = -(10nlog10d + A) \qquad (1)$$

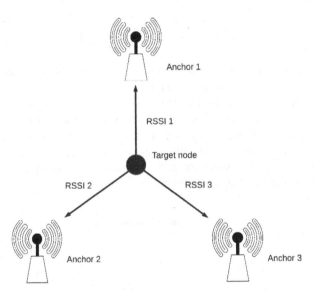

Fig. 1. System overview of the indoor localization system

2.2 RSSI Filtering

The distance between nodes is highly correlated to the RSSI value as per Eq. 1, which generally decreases as the distance between them increases and increases as the distance decreases. However, due to the instability of the RSSI value during transmission, its volatility is high. The RSSI value of a node closer to the other node may be smaller than that of a node farther away [22].

In our work, we use Gaussian models for filtering multiple RSSI values. The crucial aspect for enhancing the overall accuracy of laboratory data is the selection of data points from the high-probability region within a large set of sampled data and the elimination of events with small probabilities. This approach mitigates the impact of data volatility on experimental performance, thereby yielding more representative and stable experimental data, as well as more compelling results in positioning experiments. In general, the probability density function of a Gaussian function can be represented as follows:

$$f(x) = \frac{1}{\sqrt{2\pi}\sigma} e^{\frac{(-x-u)^2}{2\sigma^2}} \tag{2}$$

where,

$$u = \frac{1}{n} \sum\nolimits_{i=1}^{n} x_i \tag{3}$$

$$\sigma^2 = \frac{1}{1-n} \sum\nolimits_{i=1}^{n} (x_i - u)^2 \tag{4}$$

$$\sigma = \sqrt{\frac{1}{n} \sum\nolimits_{i=1}^{n} (RSSI_i - \frac{1}{n} \sum\nolimits_{i=1}^{n} RSSI_i)} \tag{5}$$

The RSSI data that was sampled underwent a filtering process based on a pre-defined value range. Any data that was found to be outside of this range was discarded, while all data within the range was retained. The RSSI values that were found to occur frequently in the high probability area were then subjected to a geometric averaging process. This resulted in obtaining RSSI values that were more representative of the communication process between the nodes [37]. The filtering process was applied to the RSSI values received from seventeen access points in the dataset. The resulting filtered dataset for selected WAPs was visualized, as shown in Fig. 2.

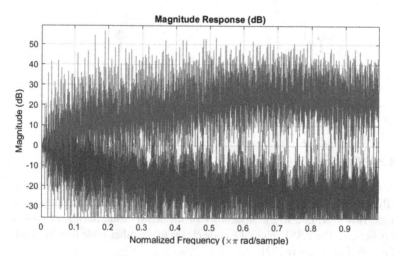

Fig. 2. RSSI dataset after filtering

3 Experiment Testbed and Dataset

In this research, we make use of the publicly available UJIIndoorLoc dataset [23]. Compared to other datasets found in the literature, this dataset contains 19,938 data points and is well-documented. It covers a total area of 108,703 m^2 and comprises three buildings, each with four or five stories. The database includes 933 distinct locations, serving as reference points. For training, we utilized 19,938 sampled points, while 1,111 points were allocated for validation and testing, making a total of 21,049 data points. To ensure dataset independence, we conducted validation (or testing) samples four months after the training ones. The dataset encompasses 520 unique wireless access points (WAPs), and data was collected using 25 different mobile device models, used by more than 20 individuals. Table 1 displays a sample extract from the WAPs list, along with their respective 14 RSSI values.

Table 1. Extract the WAPs list with 14 RSSI values [23]

Pos. in the list	WAP identifier	RSSI level
1st	WAP_{032}	-97 dBm
2nd	WAP_{001}	-97 dBm
3rd	WAP_{268}	-97 dBm
4th	WAP_{150}	-94 dBm
—		
11th	WAP_{036}	-65 dBm
12th	WAP_{035}	-65 dBm
13th	WAP_{142}	-48 dBm
14th	WAP_{143}	-46 dBm

During the pre-processing data stage, we filtered the dataset before training. This dataset consists of three buildings. Two buildings have five floors each, and one has three floors. For classification, we have assigned an ID for all 15 floors from 0 to 14, identified as the class labels where floor ID will be the targeted variable in the dataset [37].

4 Machine Learning Models

Proposed algorithms have their own strengths and weaknesses when it comes to estimating the location, and the choice of algorithm depends on the specific problem, dataset size, interpretability requirements, and computational resources available. It's crucial to consider these factors when selecting the most appropriate algorithm for a given task.

4.1 Comparison of ML Algorithms

See Table 2.

Table 2. Comparison of algorithms

Type of Algorithm	• Local Gaussian Regression: Regression algorithm that models the relationship between variables using Gaussian distributions locally • K-nearest neighbor (KNN): Instance-based classification algorithm that classifies data points based on the majority class of their k-nearest neighbors • Decision Tree Classifier: Supervised learning algorithm that builds a tree-like structure to make decisions based on feature conditions • XGBoost: Gradient boosting algorithm known for its efficiency and high predictive performance • LightGBM: Gradient boosting framework designed for efficient training with lower memory consumption • Support Vector Classifier (SVC): Classification algorithm that finds an optimal hyperplane to separate data points into different classes
Applicability	• Local Gaussian Regression: Suitable for regression tasks where the relationship between variables is locally modeled with Gaussian distributions • K-nearest neighbor: Applicable for both classification and regression tasks, particularly useful for cases with local patterns and when the data is not linearly separable • Decision Tree Classifier: Widely used for classification tasks and can handle both numerical and categorical data • XGBoost: Preferred for structured/tabular data and widely used in various machine learning competitions due to its high accuracy • LightGBM: Similar to XGBoost, suitable for structured/tabular data, but with faster training speed and lower memory usage • Support Vector Classifier: Effective for binary classification tasks and can handle high-dimensional feature spaces • Gaussian Naive Bayes: Simple and efficient, suitable for text classification and other tasks with discrete features

(continued)

Table 2. (*continued*)

Interpretability	• Local Gaussian Regression: Interpretable, as it models the relationship between variables using Gaussian distributions • K-nearest neighbor: Less interpretable, as predictions are based on the majority of neighboring data points • Decision Tree Classifier: Fairly interpretable, as the decision rules can be visualized • XGBoost: Less interpretable than Decision Trees, but feature importance can be extracted • LightGBM: Similar to XGBoost, provides feature importance information • Support Vector Classifier: Relatively interpretable with clear decision boundaries • Gaussian Naive Bayes: Interpretable, as the probabilities of each feature contribute to the final classification
Performance on Large Datasets	• Local Gaussian Regression: Computationally expensive and may not scale well to large datasets • K-nearest neighbor: Can be slow and memory-intensive on large datasets, as it needs to compute distances for all data points • Decision Tree Classifier: Fast on large datasets but may suffer from overfitting if not pruned properly • XGBoost: Efficient on large datasets, particularly designed to handle high-dimensional data • LightGBM: Faster than XGBoost on large datasets due to its binning-based approach • Support Vector Classifier: Can be slow on large datasets, especially if the data is high-dimensional • Gaussian Naive Bayes: Fast and scalable on large datasets due to its simple probabilistic nature

5 Models Training and Results

The model training and location estimation process are depicted in Fig. 3. The collected dataset was subjected to Gaussian filtering to reduce initial dataset noise. After filtering, the dataset was split into a 70% training set and a 30% test set. Python was utilized for all model training, and the model's performance was evaluated using the metrics of Accuracy, Precision, Recall, and F1 score. All the codes are available at https://github.com/isurushanaka/apan_indoorloc.

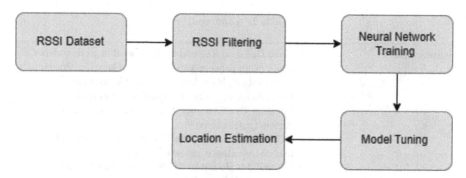

Fig. 3. Location Estimation Process

Based on the observation in Table 3, The XGB_model and LGB_model demonstrate remarkably high accuracy, precision, recall, and F1 scores, indicating their exceptional performance in the given task. On the other hand, the GNB_model appears to have relatively low accuracy and F1 score compared to the other models. The choice of the most suitable model depends on the specific requirements and constraints of the application. The XGB_model is a type of ensemble learning algorithm. The combination of ensemble learning, gradient boosting, regularization, and feature importance analysis in XGBoost makes it a powerful and versatile algorithm for indoor localization tasks, often leading to excellent accuracy compared to other algorithms (Figs. 4, 5, 6, 7, 8 and 9).

Table 3. Performance evaluation metrices.

	Model	Accuracy	Precision	Recall	F1
0	LGR_model	0.945503	0.943679	0.943495	0.943493
1	KNN_model	0.947844	0.947564	0.946257	0.946267
2	DTC_model	0.938148	0.9393	0.937152	0.938014
4	XGB_model	0.993815	0.994338	0.991095	0.992601
5	LGB_model	0.995319	0.995878	0.993069	0.994392
6	SVC_model	0.961384	0.962529	0.957508	0.959759
7	GNB_model	0.474925	0.625258	0.531785	0.455524

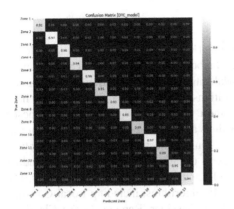

Fig. 4. Confusion Matrix for DTC

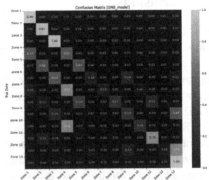

Fig. 5. Confusion Matrix for GNB

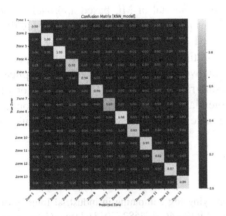

Fig. 6. Confusion Matrix for KNN

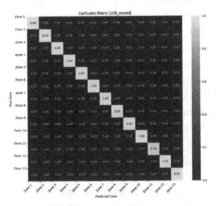

Fig. 7. Confusion Matrix for LGB

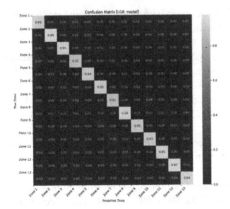

Fig. 8. Confusion Matrix for LGR

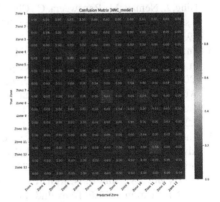

Fig. 9. Confusion Matrix for SVC

6 Conclusions

This paper introduces a novel Machine Learning (ML)-based approach for indoor localization using radio signal data. In the context of modern location-based Internet of Things (IoT) applications, precise indoor object localization is a critical requirement. The traditional probabilistic and deterministic algorithms presented in existing literature have shown limitations, prompting the need for more advanced techniques. Our proposed localization framework leverages ML algorithms and Received Signal Strength Indication (RSSI) values to estimate the indoor location of objects. To validate the effectiveness of our approach, we conducted experiments using a publicly available UCJIndoor localization dataset containing RSSI values collected from known indoor locations. The dataset allowed us to train and test various ML algorithms, including Local Gaussian Regression, K-nearest neighbor, Decision Tree Classifier, Random Forest Classifier, XGBoost, LightGBM, Support Vector Classifier, and Gaussian Naive Bayes. The experimental results revealed the superiority of XGBoost, achieving an impressive 99% accuracy in indoor localization. This highlights the potential of ML-based approaches for enhancing localization accuracy in indoor environments, thereby contributing significantly to the advancement of location-based IoT applications. By addressing the limitations of traditional algorithms and demonstrating the effectiveness of our proposed ML-based approach, this study lays the groundwork for further research and applications in the domain of indoor localization using radio signal data. The combination of ML techniques and RSSI values has the potential to revolutionize indoor positioning systems, making them more accurate and reliable for a wide range of IoT applications in various indoor environments.

References

1. Aazam, M., Zeadally, S., Harras, K.A.: Deploying fog computing in industrial Internet of Things and industry 4.0. IEEE Trans. Ind. Inf. **14**(10), 4674–4682 (2018). https://doi.org/10.1109/TII.2018.2855198
2. Ding, J., Nemati, M., Ranaweera, C., Choi, J.: IoT connectivity technologies and applications: a survey. IEEE Access **8**, 67646–67673 (2020). https://doi.org/10.1109/ACCESS.2020.2985932
3. Fu, S., Li, Z., Liu, K., Din, S., Imran, M., Yang, X.: Model compression for IoT applications in industry 4.0 via multiscale knowledge transfer. IEEE Trans. Ind. Inf. **16**(9), 6013–6022 (2020). https://doi.org/10.1109/TII.2019.2953106
4. Wu, K., Xiao, J., Yi, Y., Chen, D., Luo, X., Ni, L.M.: CSI-based indoor localization. IEEE Trans. Parallel Distrib. Syst. **24**(7), 1300–1309 (2013). https://doi.org/10.1109/TPDS.2012.214
5. Liu, X.-Y., Wang, X.: Real-time indoor localization for smartphones using tensor-generative adversarial nets. IEEE Trans. Neural Netw. Learn. Syst. **32**(8), 3433–3443 (2021). https://doi.org/10.1109/TNNLS.2020.3010724
6. Li, L., Guo, X., Ansari, N.: SmartLoc: smart wireless indoor localization empowered by machine learning. IEEE Trans. Ind. Electron. **67**(8), 6883–6893 (2020). https://doi.org/10.1109/TIE.2019.2931261
7. Xia, H., Zuo, J., Liu, S., Qiao, Y.: Indoor localization on smartphones using built-in sensors and map constraints. IEEE Trans. Instrum. Meas. **68**(4), 1189–1198 (2019). https://doi.org/10.1109/TIM.2018.2863478

8. Liu, N., He, T., He, S., Niu, Q.: Indoor localization with adaptive signal sequence representations. IEEE Trans. Veh. Technol. **70**(11), 11678–11694 (2021). https://doi.org/10.1109/TVT.2021.3113333

9. Akshay, A., Davidson, A.: A comparative analysis of localization techniques in wireless sensor network. In: 2022 IEEE International Conference on Signal Processing, Informatics, Communication and Energy Systems (SPICES), pp. 285–289 (2022). https://doi.org/10.1109/SPICES52834.2022.9774208

10. Kalyani, V.: Enhancing localization accuracy in wireless sensor networks using range-free methods and RSS measurements. In: 2018 International Conference on Recent Trends in Advance Computing (ICRTAC), pp. 136–142 (2018). https://doi.org/10.1109/ICRTAC.2018.8679291

11. Sivasakthiselvan, S., Nagarajan, V.: Localization techniques of wireless sensor networks: a review. In: 2020 International Conference on Communication and Signal Processing (ICCSP), pp. 1643–1648 (2020). https://doi.org/10.1109/ICCSP48568.2020.9182290

12. Pană, C., Severi, S., de Abreu, G.T.F.: Super-accurate source localization via multiple measurement vectors and compressed sensing techniques. In: 2018 IEEE Wireless Communications and Networking Conference (WCNC), pp. 1–5 (2018). https://doi.org/10.1109/WCNC.2018.8377451

13. Zargelin, O.A., Lashhab, F.M., Hasan, W.K.: Localization methods based on error analysis and modeling in two dimensions. In: 2020 11th IEEE Annual Ubiquitous Computing, Electronics & Mobile Communication Conference (UEMCON), pp. 0690–0699 (2020). https://doi.org/10.1109/UEMCON51285.2020.9298171

14. Hu, Y., Liu, J., Zhang, B.: Localization using blind RSS measurements. IEEE Wirel. Commun. Lett. **8**(2), 464–467 (2019). https://doi.org/10.1109/LWC.2018.2876319

15. Bharadwaj, R., Alomainy, A., Koul, S.K.: Experimental investigation of body-centric indoor localization using compact wearable antennas and machine learning algorithms. IEEE Trans. Antennas Propag. **70**(2), 1344–1354 (2022). https://doi.org/10.1109/TAP.2021.3111308

16. Zhou, C., Liu, J., Sheng, M., Zheng, Y., Li, J.: Exploiting fingerprint correlation for fingerprint-based indoor localization: a deep learning based approach. IEEE Trans. Veh. Technol. **70**(6), 5762–5774 (2021). https://doi.org/10.1109/TVT.2021.3075539

17. Nessa, A., Adhikari, B., Hussain, F., Fernando, X.N.: A survey of machine learning for indoor positioning. IEEE Access **8**, 214945–214965 (2020). https://doi.org/10.1109/ACCESS.2020.3039271

18. Gadhgadhi, A., Hachaïchi, Y., Zairi, H.: A machine learning based indoor localization. In: 2020 4th International Conference on Advanced Systems and Emergent Technologies (IC_ASET), pp. 33–38 (2020). https://doi.org/10.1109/IC_ASET49463.2020.9318284

19. Singh, N., Choe, S., Punmiya, R.: Machine learning based indoor localization using Wi-Fi RSSI fingerprints: an overview. IEEE Access **9**, 127150–127174 (2021). https://doi.org/10.1109/ACCESS.2021.3111083

20. Bozkurt, S., Elibol, G., Gunal, S., Yayan, U.: A comparative study on machine learning algorithms for indoor positioning. In: 2015 International Symposium on Innovations in Intelligent SysTems and Applications (INISTA), pp. 1–8 (2015). https://doi.org/10.1109/INISTA.2015.7276725

21. Weerasinghe, Y.S.P., Maduranga, M.W.P., Dissanayake, M.B.: RSSI and feed forward neural network (FFNN) based indoor localization in WSN. In: 2019 National Information Technology Conference (NITC), pp. 35–40 (2019). https://doi.org/10.1109/NITC48475.2019.9114515

22. Maduranga, M.W.P., Abeysekera, R.: Bluetooth low energy (BLE) and feed forward neural network (FFNN) based indoor positioning for location-based IoT applications. Int. J. Wirel. Microw. Technol. (IJWMT), **12**(2), 33–39 (2022). https://doi.org/10.5815/ijwmt.2022.02.03
23. Torres-Sospedra, J., Rambla, D., Montoliu, R., Belmonte, O., Huerta, J.: UJIIndoorLoc-Mag: a new database for magnetic field-based localization problems. In: Proceedings of the Sixth International Conference on Indoor Positioning and Indoor Navigation (IPIN 2015), Banff, Alberta, Canada 13–16 October 2015 (2015)

Illuminating the Roads: Night-to-Day Image Translation for Improved Visibility at Night

H. K. I. S. Lakmal[1]([✉])[iD] and M. B. Dissanayake[2][iD]

[1] Department of Mechatronic and Industry Engineering, NSBM Green University, Homagama, Sri Lanka
isuru.l@nsbm.ac.lk,isurushanakalakmal@gmail.com
[2] Department of Electrical and Electronic Engineering, University of Peradeniya, Peradeniya, Sri Lanka
maheshid@eng.pdn.ac.lk

Abstract. Image enhancement and night-to-day image translation are the most prominent approaches for improving visibility at night. Yet, the capability of improving visibility using image enhancement techniques, such as gamma correction, is limited. On the other hand, translating night-time images into day-time images has more potential and modern deep learning techniques such as Variational Auto Encoders (VAEs) and Generative Adversarial Networks (GAN) can be utilized for this purpose. This study focuses on exploring the possibility of achieving night-to-day image translation with a supervised GAN. To enable the training of a supervised GAN model, the availability of a pixel-to-pixel paired night-day image dataset is crucial. Hence, a pixel-to-pixel paired night-day image dataset was generated by pairing through synthesis using an existing pre-trained model. Subsequently, the proposed supervised GAN model was trained on the generated dataset. To facilitate a comprehensive comparison, a well-established pre-trained night-to-day image translation model from ToDayGAN was selected as the benchmark. According to the comparison analysis, the supervised GAN model provided 16.32 dB of average Peak-Signal to Noise Ratio (PSNR) improvement, 0.513 of average Structural Similarity Index (SSIM) improvement, 0.061 of average Inception Score (IS) improvement and 67.33 of average Fréchet Inception Distance (FID) reduction compared to the ToDayGAN night-to-day image translation model.

Keywords: Image translation · Night driving · Supervised · GAN · Road safety

1 Introduction

Driving at night can pose a significant challenge due to low-light conditions [32]. The diminished visibility during nighttime poses a significant risk and is considered one of the primary factors contributing to accidents. [14]. There are several

---

Supported by L. K. Domain Registry - Prof. V. K. Samaranayake Research Grant.

D. Herath et al. (Eds.): APANConf 2023, CCIS 1995, pp. 13–26, 2024.
https://doi.org/10.1007/978-3-031-51135-6_2

measures that can be taken to minimize the challenges of driving at night in dimly lit settings. One approach is to develop modern Advanced Driver Assistance Systems (ADAS) that can leverage different sensors to provide real-time information to drivers, allowing them to navigate the road in low-light environments better [31,33]. Another approach is to improve the visibility for drives by developing computer vision models that can transform images captured at night into resembling day-time images [20,43]. The first approach utilized visual sensors coupled with non-visual sensors such as radar sensors [15,24], infrared and thermal sensors [8,29,30], laser scanners and millimetre-wave sensors [4,6] and Radio Frequency Identification (RFID) techniques [5]. The second approach (i.e. image enhancement techniques) can be separated into night-time image enhancement [1,7,9,11,19,37,38,40] and Night-to-Day (N2D) image translation [2,3,35]. Even though there is a multitude of research on night-time image enhancement, research focused on N2D image translation is limited due to certain challenges in that approach. However, there are few studies that are focused on N2D image translation [16,17].

Most of the image translation approaches utilizes either a Variational Auto Encoders (VAE) [18,26,27,47] or a Generative Adversarial Networks (GAN) [10,12,22,23,46]. Due to the inherent capability of the GANs to produce more effective results in this domain, it has become a popular choice for image translation even though it is more challenging to train a GAN. In the context of cross-domain image translation, the GANs are classified into two groups based on their training approach: supervised and unsupervised models. The supervised models require pixel-to-pixel paired images. In contrast, unsupervised models require only two different sets of images in two different domains and pixel-to-pixel pairing among images is not required. This study aims to investigate the possibility of the N2D image translation with a supervised GAN model.

The most demanding task in the training of a supervised GAN model is acquiring a pixel-to-pixel paired dataset. Given the challenges associated with collecting night-day paired driving datasets in dynamic and unpredictable settings like roads, this study leverages a pre-trained model to synthesize night-time images for real day-time images (i.e. day-to-night image transformation). Each synthesized night-time image is paired with a corresponding day-time image resulting in a dataset consisting of corresponding night-time and day-time image pairs that are aligned at the pixel level. Further, the synthesized dataset was validated with locally collected real images before moving on to the model training stage. The training was conducted using the Pix2Pix model [10] with few customizations. After the training, the performance of the model was critically evaluated. The aim of the research presented is to find a high-performing image correction method to convert the images captured during night-time driving to a representation similar to the day-time images for better visual inspection. The experiments were carried out with the customized Pix2Pix model to achieve a high level of output image quality, thereby demonstrating the effectiveness and applicability of the proposed approach for N2D image translation.

2   Related Works

Most of the night-day image translation studies have utilized unsupervised GAN models inherently due to the challenges in acquiring pixel-to-pixel paired image dataset in a dynamic environment such as driving conditions. Commonly they are implemented as a part of an object detection task [3,35,45], an image localization task [2,45] or a semantic segmentation task [39,45]. There are different types of unsupervised GAN architectures such as Cycle-GAN [46], UNIT [26], DualGAN [44] and BicycleGAN [47] for cross-domain image translation. The Cycle-GAN architecture is frequently seen in night to day image translation studies [3,21,36,39]. UNIT is also an often used architecture [26,34,35] for cross-domain image translation.

Besides the above-stated unsupervised GAN models trained with unpaired night-day images, the model presented in [42] is trained on coarsely aligned night-day image pairs in a semi-supervised manner. When it comes to the supervised GAN models [28] has been trained as a supervised model for N2D image translation.

In summary, it can be observed that the utilization of supervised models for N2D image translation is lacking in the literature. The key reason for this lacking is the unavailability of pixel-to-pixel paired night-day datasets for training supervised models. As a contribution to this research gap, this study proposes to synthesize a night-day paired image dataset and then investigates the possibility of training a supervised N2D image translation model with the synthesized dataset.

3   Methodology

3.1   Dataset

Dataset Preparation: The initial step of compiling the dataset involved collecting a set of day-time images, which were subsequently transformed into night-time images to generate the corresponding paired dataset. First, the day-time images were acquired from publicly available benchmark datasets: Oxford RobotCar dataset [41], and ZJU dataset [39]. Next, the collected images were preprocessed by resizing them to a resolution of 256×256 pixels. To generate corresponding night-time images for every day-time image in the dataset, a pre-trained day-to-night transformation model, namely ToDayGAN [2], was utilized.

ToDayGAN is one of the state-of-the-art models which contains a day-to-night image translation. Since this is a GAN architecture, it consists of a generator network and a discriminator network. The generator network is trained to generate realistic night-time images from day-time images, while the discriminator network is trained to distinguish between real and fake night-time images. Experimental results demonstrate that the ToDayGAN model is capable of producing high-quality night-time images. Moreover, ToDayGAN has been

extensively used for comparative analysis in several cross-domain image translation studies [13, 25, 45]. Therefore the day-to-night image translation model of
ToDayGAN, with its pre-trained weights, was used for synthesizing night-time
images of the input day-time images in this research.

Once the corresponding night-time image was synthesized for every day-time
image in the dataset, they were paired to compile the final dataset. Selected sample images from the completed dataset are illustrated in Fig. 1. Further details
of generating this pixel-to-pixel paired night-day image dataset is available at
https://github.com/isurushanaka/paired-N2D.

Dataset Validation. Even though the visual observation confirms that the
dataset prepared is of desired visual quality, further validation was carried out
using a locally collected paired dataset.

In this step, a smaller yet, separate dataset of paired night-day images was
collected locally with controlled environmental parameters. The day-time images
of this local dataset were subjected to the same dataset preparation process as
earlier and paired night-time images were generated using the same ToDayGAN
model used in Sect. 3.1. Subsequently, a comparison was made between the collected night-time images and the synthesized night-time images to assess their
similarity. It was carried out using the two widely used image quality evaluation
metrics, the Structural Similarity Index (SSIM) and the Peak Signal-to-Noise
Ratio (PSNR). The SSIM evaluates the resemblance between the two images in
terms of image structure, as it foresees the impact of image structure on Human
Visual Systems (HVS), whereas the PSNR metric measures the variations in
colour scale by providing a quantitative assessment of their fidelity in terms of
colour representation.

To facilitate a meaningful comparison, night-time images generated by
ToDayGAN, are compared against the night-time images synthesized by another
benchmark pre-trained model from [16, 17] which uses a Cycle-GAN [46]. Figure 2
shows random samples of generated night images from both models, against the

Fig. 1. Samples of the pixel-to-pixel paired night-day image dataset generated using
TodayGAN.

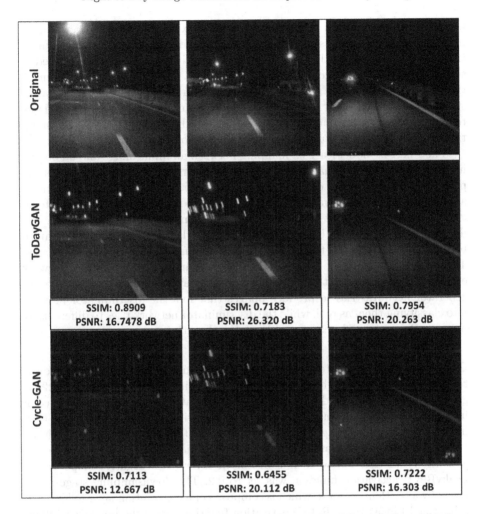

Fig. 2. Comparison of original natural local night-time images with the night-time images synthesized by ToDayGAN and the Cycle-GAN. The SSIM and PSNR values of each generated image are indicated below the image itself.

locally collected night images. It was observed that the average SSIM index and the average PSNR of the images generated by the TodayGAN model are respectively 13.3% and 22.5% higher than those generated by the Cycle-GAN model. This suggests that the images generated by the ToDayGAN model were able to retain the quality and the structural similarity in the synthesized images.

3.2   GAN-Model

After acquiring the pixel-to-pixel paired dataset, a suitable supervised image translation model was selected next. Even though there are many supervised image translation models in the literature, the Pix2Pix model [10] stands apart from the others due to its versatility in accommodating various types of image translations with paired data. These applications include but are not limited to semantic segmentation, edge-to-image translation, and image-to-image translation and it has served as a reference for numerous cross-domain image translation studies. Further, the light weight of the model is an advantage for real-time systems like ADAS. Therefore, in the presented study the supervised N2D image translation was explored using a customized version of the Pix2Pix model.

The Pix2Pix model learns a mapping between an input image and an output image based on paired image data. The architecture of the model comprises two parts: a generator and a discriminator. The generator receives an input image and produces an output image that is conditioned on the input. The generator is trained to produce output images that closely resemble ground truth images. The discriminator network is based on a PatchGAN classifier [10], which is trained to differentiate between the generated images and the ground truth images. Throughout the training, the generator network and the discriminator network engage in a simultaneous training process, while playing a min-max game. i.e. the generator network tries to produce images that fool the discriminator network into classifying them as real, while the discriminator network tries to differentiate between the generated images and the ground truth images.

Generator. The generator (G) utilized in this study is a customized version of the Pix2Pix generator. This is also a U-network similar to the original Pix2Pix generator with minor modifications to accommodate input ($256 \times 256 \times 3$) color images and produce output ($256 \times 256 \times 3$) color images. It receives night-time images as the input and gradually downsamples it through several convolution layers. A batch normalization and a Leaky Rectified Linear Unit (LeakyReLU) activation function follow each convolution layer. The negative slope of the LeakyReLU activation function was set to 0.2. The downsampling stage is followed by a bottleneck block, which is composed of a convolution layer followed by a Rectified Linear Unit (ReLU) activation function. After the bottleneck block, the generator gradually upsamples the image back to its original dimensions through several transposed convolution layers. Transposed convolution layers are followed by batch normalization and a ReLU activation function. The first three blocks in the upsampling stage contain three dropout layers with 0.5 probability. Moreover, layers from the downsampling stage are combined with the layer from the upsampling stage through skip connections, allowing the high-level information to be propagated through the model. Construction of the customized generator architecture is illustrated in Fig. 3.

Discriminator. The discriminator (D) utilized in this experiment is a 70×70 PatchGAN classifier from the original Pix2Pix which attempts to classify each 70×70 pixel section in an image as either real or fake. The discriminator in PatchGAN runs convolutionally over each image, averaging all responses. The output of the final convolution layer of the discriminator is forwarded through a sigmoid function, which maps the output between 0 and 1. The value 0 indicates that the corresponding patch is fake and 1 indicates that it is real. According to the study presented in [10], the output of the 70×70 GAN is sharp in both spatial and spectral domains. The construction discriminator architecture is illustrated in Fig. 3.

Training Objective. The training objective of the Pix2Pix consists of two main components: the adversarial loss and the pixel-wise reconstruction loss. The adversarial loss encourages the generator to improve its image synthesis capabilities by minimizing the ability of the discriminator to distinguish between the synthesized and real images. The pixel-wise reconstruction loss function quantifies the disparity between the generated images and the corresponding real images on a pixel level. It ensures that the generated output closely matches the desired target image, enhancing the visual fidelity and preserving fine details [10]. The pixel-wise reconstruction loss used in this study is the L1 loss. By optimizing both the adversarial loss and the pixel-wise reconstruction loss, the model can learn to synthesize high-quality and visually plausible outputs. Let $x \in X$ represent night-time images, $y \in Y$ represent day-time images and $z \in Z$ represent random noise vectors (from Gaussian Noise Distribution). During the training process, the discriminator aims to differentiate the day-time images synthesized by the generator (i.e. $G(x, z)$) from y while the generator aims to synthesize day-time images $G(x, z)$ indistinguishable from y. The adversarial loss and the L1 loss associated with the Pix2Pix training are indicated in the Eq. 1 and the Eq. 2 respectively.

$$L_{cGAN}(G, D) = \mathbf{E}_y[\log(D(y))] + \mathbf{E}_{x,z}[1 - \log(D(G(x, z)))] \qquad (1)$$

$$L_{L1}(G) = \mathbf{E}_{x,y,z}[\|y - G(x, z)\|_1] \qquad (2)$$

3.3 Training

The proposed architecture was implemented using Python 3.9.7 and the PyTorch framework. The experiment was simulated on a Dell OptiPlex 5080 computer equipped with an Intel Core i7-10700 CPU 2.9GHz processor, and 16384MB RAM. Hardware acceleration for training was achieved using the NVIDIA GeForce GTX 1660 SUPER GPU. The training process took place over a duration of 2 days. When training the model, the learning rate was set as 0.0001 and trained for 300 epochs. The Adam optimizer was used for the optimization. The model was trained in batches with a batch size of 8.

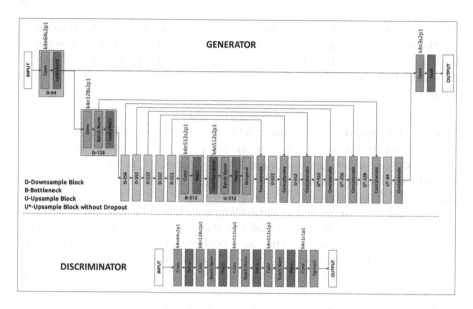

Fig. 3. Architecture of the discriminator and the customized generator of the Pix2Pix model.

4   Results and Discussion

4.1   Evaluation Metrics

PSNR. PSNR is a commonly used objective quality evaluation metric for images. It is defined as the ratio of the maximum possible power of the image to the power of the difference between the original and reconstructed images. A higher PSNR value indicates lower levels of distortion and higher quality of the reconstructed image. PSNR provides a quantitative measure in terms of the reconstruction quality, colour accuracy brightness and contrast.

SSIM. PSNR only considers pixel-level differences and does not take into account other aspects of image quality, such as structural information, texture, and semantic content. Therefore, the SSIM is introduced as another evaluation metric which assesses the similarity between two images by taking into account more aspects of image quality, such as luminance, contrast, and structure.

Inception Score (IS). IS is a performance evaluation metric commonly used in GANs. It evaluates the quality and diversity of the generated images by considering two aspects: the marginal probability of the generated image classes and the conditional probability of the generated images given their corresponding classes. A higher IS score indicates that the generated images have high quality and diversity.

Fréchet Inception Distance (FID). Since the IS is influenced by the architecture of the generator network, the choice of classes, and the training process, it alone is not considered a perfect metric. Therefore, Frechet Inception Distance (FID) is used to complement IS which provides a more comprehensive evaluation of the generated images. It provides a measure of the distance between the feature representations of the generated images and the real images in an abstract feature space. A lower FID score indicates that the generated images are more similar to the real images, and therefore have higher quality.

4.2   Comparison Analysis

A comprehensive analysis of the image quality of the synthesized day images, of the customized Pix2Pix model was carried out with four evaluation metrics. To establish a baseline framework for comparison, a pre-trained N2D image translation model from ToDayGAN was employed. The rationale behind using the ToDayGAN model as a baseline lies in the fact that the dataset used to train our customized Pix2Pix model was synthesized using the day-to-night image translation model from ToDayGAN. By comparing the performance of our customized Pix2Pix model against the pre-trained N2D image translation ToDay-GAN model, we aim to determine whether our model can achieve superior results in N2D image translation. This comparative analysis provided valuable insight into the potential advancements and effectiveness of our customized Pix2Pix model. Furthermore, to conduct a comprehensive analysis and study in light of recent work, we also selected Cycle-GAN [16] N2D image translation model as a benchmark for comparison with our model. According to the evaluation metric scores, indicated in Table 1, it can be clearly observed that our customized Pix2Pix model has outperformed the ToDayGAN model in N2D image translation. Sample images synthesized by both models and their evaluation metric scores are indicated in Fig. 4 for visual comparison.

5   Conclusion

This study explores the possibility of achieving N2D image translation using a supervised GAN. Since it is required to have a pixel-to-pixel paired night-day image dataset to train a supervised GAN, this study compiles such a dataset by synthesizing paired night-time images for a given day-time images using a pre-trained day-to-night (D2N) image translation model from ToDayGAN. Then a customized Pix2Pix model was trained using the dataset generated following the

Table 1. Evaluation scores of the Pix2Pix.

Model	Avg. PSNR (dB) ↑	Avg. SSIM ↑	Inception Score ↑	FID ↓
Pix2Pix	27.6321	0.8119	2.8291	95.243
ToDayGAN (N2D) [2]	11.3126	0.3164	2.7685	162.569
Cycle-GAN (N2D) [16]	13.4113	0.6422	2.5943	106.332

supervised GAN training approach. A pre-trained N2D image translation model from ToDayGAN was selected as the benchmark to compare the performance of our trained Pix2Pix model. By comparing the performance of the customized Pix2Pix model against the pre-trained ToDayGAN model, we aim to determine whether the customized Pix2Pix model can achieve superior results in N2D image translation. According to the comparison analysis, results of the trained Pix2Pix model achieved 16.32 dB of average PSNR improvement, 0.513 of average SSIM improvement, 0.0606 of average IS improvement and 67.33 of average FID reduction compared to the ToDayGAN model. Even though the trained model is capable of synthesizing higher-quality images for the compiled dataset, it is important to explore the possibility of adapting this trained model for different night-time driving environments. Figure 5 showcases examples of translating local night-time images using our model. It is evident from the results that the

Fig. 4. Comparison of sample images synthesized by the customized Pix2Pix and the ToDayGAN N2D images translation model. The SSIM, PSNR and FID scores of each generated image are indicated below the image itself.

Fig. 5. Translation of local night-time images.

model may require fine-tuning for different driving environments. Additionally, as future work it is important to evaluate the supervised approach against different unsupervised methods to reveal the strengths and weaknesses of both approaches and assess their effectiveness and generalizability.

References

1. Acharya, U.K., Kumar, S.: Image enhancement using exposure and standard deviation-based sub-image histogram equalization for night-time images. In: Bansal, P., Tushir, M., Balas, V.E., Srivastava, R. (eds.) Proceedings of International Conference on Artificial Intelligence and Applications. AISC, vol. 1164, pp. 607–615. Springer, Singapore (2021). https://doi.org/10.1007/978-981-15-4992-2_57
2. Anoosheh, A., Sattler, T., Timofte, R., Pollefeys, M., Van Gool, L.: Night-to-day image translation for retrieval-based localization. In: 2019 International Conference on Robotics and Automation (ICRA), pp. 5958–5964. IEEE (2019)
3. Arruda, V.F., et al.: Cross-domain car detection using unsupervised image-to-image translation: From day to night. In: 2019 International Joint Conference on Neural Networks (IJCNN), pp. 1–8. IEEE (2019)
4. Etinger, A., Balal, N., Litvak, B., Einat, M., Kapilevich, B., Pinhasi, Y.: Non-imaging mm-wave FMCW sensor for pedestrian detection. IEEE Sens. J. **14**(4), 1232–1237 (2013)
5. Forczmański, P., Małecki, K.: Selected aspects of traffic signs recognition: visual versus RFID approach. In: International Conference on Transport Systems Telematics, pp. 268–274. Springer (2013)
6. Gidel, S., Checchin, P., Blanc, C., Chateau, T., Trassoudaine, L.: Pedestrian detection and tracking in an urban environment using a multilayer laser scanner. IEEE Trans. Intell. Transp. Syst. **11**(3), 579–588 (2010)
7. Guo, H., Xu, W., Qiu, S.: Unsupervised low-light image enhancement with quality-task-perception loss. In: 2021 International Joint Conference on Neural Networks (IJCNN), pp. 1–8. IEEE (2021)

8. Heo, D., Lee, E., Ko, B.C.: Pedestrian detection at night using deep neural networks and saliency maps. Electron. Imaging **30**, 1–9 (2018)
9. Hu, H., Cao, W., Yuan, J., Yang, J.: A low-illumination image enhancement algorithm based on morphological-retinex (MR) operator. In: 2021 IEEE/ACIS 6th International Conference on Big Data, Cloud Computing, and Data Science (BCD), pp. 66–72. IEEE (2021)
10. Isola, P., Zhu, J.Y., Zhou, T., Efros, A.A.: Image-to-image translation with conditional adversarial networks. In: Proceedings of the IEEE Conference on Computer Vision and Pattern Recognition, pp. 1125–1134 (2017)
11. Jiang, X., Yao, H., Liu, D.: Nighttime image enhancement based on image decomposition. SIViP **13**(1), 189–197 (2019)
12. Kazemi, H., Soleymani, S., Taherkhani, F., Iranmanesh, S., Nasrabadi, N.: Unsupervised image-to-image translation using domain-specific variational information bound. In: Advances in Neural Information Processing Systems, vol. 31 (2018)
13. Kim, D., Shin, S., Park, J., Shin, S.: Development of a semantic scene conversion model for image-based localization at night. In: Proceedings of the Conference on Research in Adaptive and Convergent Systems, pp. 107–112 (2019)
14. Konstantopoulos, P., Chapman, P., Crundall, D.: Driver's visual attention as a function of driving experience and visibility. using a driving simulator to explore drivers' eye movements in day, night and rain driving. Accid. Anal. Prevent. **42**(3), 827–834 (2010)
15. Kowol, K., Rottmann, M., Bracke, S., Gottschalk, H.: Yodar: Uncertainty-based sensor fusion for vehicle detection with camera and radar sensors. arXiv preprint arXiv:2010.03320 (2020)
16. Lakmal, H., Dissanayake, M.B.: Improving the visibility at night for advanced driver assistance systems using night-to-day image translation. In: 2022 6th SLAAI International Conference on Artificial Intelligence (SLAAI-ICAI), pp. 1–6. IEEE (2022)
17. Lakmal, H., Dissanayake, M.: Improving visibility at night with cross domain image translation for advance driver assistance systems (2022)
18. Lee, H.-Y., Tseng, H.-Y., Huang, J.-B., Singh, M., Yang, M.-H.: Diverse image-to-image translation via disentangled representations. In: Ferrari, V., Hebert, M., Sminchisescu, C., Weiss, Y. (eds.) ECCV 2018. LNCS, vol. 11205, pp. 36–52. Springer, Cham (2018). https://doi.org/10.1007/978-3-030-01246-5_3
19. Li, G., Yang, Y., Qu, X., Cao, D., Li, K.: A deep learning based image enhancement approach for autonomous driving at night. Knowl. Based Syst. **213**, 106617 (2021)
20. Li, W., Liu, X., Yuan, Y.: Sigma++: improved semantic-complete graph matching for domain adaptive object detection. IEEE Trans. Pattern Anal. Mach. Intell. **45**, 9022–9040 (2023)
21. Li, X., Guo, X., Zhang, J.: N2d-GAN: a night-to-day image-to-image translator. In: 2022 IEEE International Conference on Multimedia and Expo (ICME), pp. 1–6. IEEE (2022)
22. Lin, J., Pang, Y., Xia, Y., Chen, Z., Luo, J.: TuiGAN: learning versatile image-to-image translation with two unpaired images. In: Vedaldi, A., Bischof, H., Brox, T., Frahm, J.-M. (eds.) ECCV 2020. LNCS, vol. 12349, pp. 18–35. Springer, Cham (2020). https://doi.org/10.1007/978-3-030-58548-8_2
23. Lin, J., Xia, Y., Liu, S., Zhao, S., Chen, Z.: ZstGAN: an adversarial approach for unsupervised zero-shot image-to-image translation. Neurocomputing **461**, 327–335 (2021)
24. Lisheng, J., Lei, C., Bo, C.: Leading vehicle detection at night based on millimeter-wave radar and machine vision. J. Autom. Saf. Energy **7**(02), 167 (2016)

25. Liu, L., Cappelle, C., Ruichek, Y.: Day and night place recognition based on low-quality night-time images. In: 2020 IEEE 23rd International Conference on Intelligent Transportation Systems (ITSC), pp. 1–6. IEEE (2020)
26. Liu, M.Y., Breuel, T., Kautz, J.: Unsupervised image-to-image translation networks. In: Advances in Neural Information Processing Systems, vol. 30 (2017)
27. Ma, L., Jia, X., Georgoulis, S., Tuytelaars, T., Van Gool, L.: Exemplar guided unsupervised image-to-image translation with semantic consistency. arXiv preprint arXiv:1805.11145 (2018)
28. Meng, Y., Kong, D., Zhu, Z., Zhao, Y.: From night to day: GANs based low quality image enhancement. Neural Process. Lett. **50**(1), 799–814 (2019)
29. Nanda, H., Davis, L.: Probabilistic template based pedestrian detection in infrared videos. In: Intelligent Vehicle Symposium, 2002, vol. 1, pp. 15–20. IEEE (2002)
30. Nowosielski, A., Małecki, K., Forczmański, P., Smoliński, A.: Pedestrian detection in severe lighting conditions: comparative study of human performance vs thermal-imaging-based automatic system. In: Burduk, R., Kurzynski, M., Wozniak, M. (eds.) CORES 2019. AISC, vol. 977, pp. 174–183. Springer, Cham (2020). https://doi.org/10.1007/978-3-030-19738-4_18
31. Ogawa, T., Sakai, H., Suzuki, Y., Takagi, K., Morikawa, K.: Pedestrian detection and tracking using in-vehicle lidar for automotive application. In: 2011 IEEE Intelligent Vehicles Symposium (IV), pp. 734–739. IEEE (2011)
32. Owens, D.A., Wood, J.M., Owens, J.M.: Effects of age and illumination on night driving: a road test. Hum. Factors **49**(6), 1115–1131 (2007)
33. Rashed, H., Ramzy, M., Vaquero, V., El Sallab, A., Sistu, G., Yogamani, S.: Fusemodnet: Real-time camera and lidar based moving object detection for robust low-light autonomous driving. In: Proceedings of the IEEE/CVF International Conference on Computer Vision Workshops (2019)
34. Romera, E., Bergasa, L.M., Yang, K., Alvarez, J.M., Barea, R.: Bridging the day and night domain gap for semantic segmentation. In: 2019 IEEE Intelligent Vehicles Symposium (IV), pp. 1312–1318. IEEE (2019)
35. Schutera, M., Hussein, M., Abhau, J., Mikut, R., Reischl, M.: Night-to-day: online image-to-image translation for object detection within autonomous driving by night. IEEE Trans. Intell. Veh. **6**(3), 480–489 (2020)
36. Shiotsuka, D., et al.: Gan-based semantic-aware translation for day-to-night images. In: 2022 IEEE International Conference on Consumer Electronics (ICCE), pp. 1–6. IEEE (2022)
37. Singh, A., et al.: Interpretable classification of human exercise videos through pose estimation and multivariate time series analysis. In: Shaban-Nejad, A., Michalowski, M., Bianco, S. (eds.) AI for Disease Surveillance and Pandemic Intelligence. W3PHAI 2021. Studies in Computational Intelligence, vol. 1013, pp. 181–199. Springer, Cham (2021). https://doi.org/10.1007/978-3-030-93080-6_14
38. Sparavigna, A.C.: Night image enhancement by means of retinex filtering (2020)
39. Sun, L., Wang, K., Yang, K., Xiang, K.: See clearer at night: towards robust nighttime semantic segmentation through day-night image conversion. In: Artificial Intelligence and Machine Learning in Defense Applications, vol. 11169, p. 111690A. International Society for Optics and Photonics (2019)
40. Turan, B.: A image enhancement method for night-way images. Balkan J. Elect. Comput. Eng. **9**(1), 8–16 (2021)
41. Vi, W., Maddern, G., Pascoe, C., Linegar, N.P.: 1 year 1000 km. The Oxford robotcar dataset. Int. J. Robot. Res. **36**(1), 3–15 (2017)

42. Xia, Y., Monica, J., Chao, W.L., Hariharan, B., Weinberger, K.Q., Campbell, M.: Image-to-image translation for autonomous driving from coarsely-aligned image pairs. arXiv preprint arXiv:2209.11673 (2022)

43. Yang, C., Liu, Y., Zell, A.: Learning-based camera relocalization with domain adaptation via image-to-image translation. In: 2021 International Conference on Unmanned Aircraft Systems (ICUAS), pp. 1047–1054. IEEE (2021)

44. Yi, Z., Zhang, H., Tan, P., Gong, M.: DualGAN: unsupervised dual learning for image-to-image translation. In: Proceedings of the IEEE International Conference on Computer Vision, pp. 2849–2857 (2017)

45. Zheng, Z., Wu, Y., Han, X., Shi, J.: ForkGAN: seeing into the rainy night. In: Vedaldi, A., Bischof, H., Brox, T., Frahm, J.-M. (eds.) ECCV 2020. LNCS, vol. 12348, pp. 155–170. Springer, Cham (2020). https://doi.org/10.1007/978-3-030-58580-8_10

46. Zhu, J.Y., Park, T., Isola, P., Efros, A.A.: Unpaired image-to-image translation using cycle-consistent adversarial networks. In: Proceedings of the IEEE International Conference on Computer Vision, pp. 2223–2232 (2017)

47. Zhu, J.Y., et al.: Toward multimodal image-to-image translation. In: Advances in Neural Information Processing Systems, vol. 30 (2017)

Predicting the Smear Conversion of Pulmonary Tuberculosis Patients Using Machine Learning

Ravindu Pathirana[1]($\boxtimes$), Anusha Jayasiri[2], and Thanuja Tissera[2]

[1] University of Kelaniya, Colombo 11600, Sri Lanka
`pathiran_ps17136@stu.kln.ac.lk`
[2] Department of Statistics and Computer Science, Colombo 11600, Sri Lanka
`anusha.j@vpa.ac.lk`

Abstract. This paper presents the development and evaluation of a neural network model for predicting the after-treatment smear status in a medical context. The dataset comprised demographic variables, X-ray image results, and the smear status after the intensive phase. To address the data imbalance, the SMOTE technique was employed. Significant variables were selected through correlation analysis and feature selection, leading to the construction of a neural network model with specific parameters. The model was trained on a 70% training dataset using 3-fold cross-validation and achieved an accuracy of 90.80% after 400 epochs. Model evaluation and validation on the remaining 30% of the testing dataset demonstrated its effectiveness in accurately classifying positive and negative smear statuses. The precision, recall, and F1-scores for both classes indicated balanced performance. The model's reliability in predicting smear status is supported by the heatmap analysis. Future work includes further validation on larger and more diverse datasets, consideration of potential limitations, and exploration of advanced techniques like deep learning. The developed neural network model shows promise in clinical applications and can contribute to improved decision-making in the treatment of patients.

Keywords: Pulmonary Tuberculosis · Neural Network · Machine Learning

1 Introduction

A highly infectious bacterial infection known as tuberculosis (TB) is carried on by Mycobacterium tuberculosis (MTB) [1]. It is transmitted through inhaling tiny droplets containing the bacteria from infected individuals. The World Health Organization (WHO) [2] claims that TB, which affects millions of people annually, is a serious worldwide health issue. Common symptoms of active TB include chest pains, fever, weight loss, weakness, night sweats, and a persistent cough [3]. Diagnosing TB promptly is crucial to prevent its spread and ensure effective treatment. Smear conversion, the transition from positive to negative sputum culture for MTB, is an important indicator of treatment effectiveness and patient non-contagiousness.

Machine learning is a rapidly evolving field within artificial intelligence that focuses on developing algorithms and models capable of learning from data [4]. By analyzing complex patterns and relationships within datasets, machine learning enables computers to make predictions and informed decisions without explicit programming. It has the ability to handle large volumes of data, extract valuable insights, and automate data analysis processes. Machine learning algorithms are applicable to various industries and have the potential to revolutionize decision-making processes.

A significant subset of machine learning models called artificial neural networks (ANNs) are modeled after the structure and operation of the human brain [5]. ANNs consist of interconnected artificial neurons organized into layers, including input and output layers, as well as hidden layers. Neural networks excel at recognizing non-linear correlations within data, enabling them to capture complex relationships that may be challenging to define explicitly. They learn from data through a training process, adjusting the weights associated with each input to optimize their predictions. Neural networks offer flexibility and can be tailored to specific tasks and data sources.

The goal of the work is to specifically create a prediction model that can estimate the chance of smear conversion [3] (positive to negative or vice versa) at two months based on the Chest X-Ray (CXR) results and clinical data. By automating this prediction process, healthcare professionals can make informed decisions regarding treatment plans and resource allocation, leading to more efficient patient management and improved outcomes. Also, it aims to achieve several subsidiary objectives. It can serve as an aid for doctors in creating follow-up plans based on priority, identify patients who may require additional guidance at an early stage, and facilitate efficient patient follow-up. The findings of this study have the potential to enhance TB treatment strategies and patient care by providing valuable insights and aiding in decision-making processes.

2 Background

Pulmonary tuberculosis (PTB) is a significant global health concern, affecting millions of individuals worldwide and causing substantial morbidity and mortality, particularly in developing countries [6]. Accurate monitoring of treatment response is a challenge in PTB management, and smear conversion, which indicates the absence of acid-fast bacilli on sputum microscopy, is a crucial indicator of treatment effectiveness and clinical outcomes. However, the standard method of sputum microscopy for smear conversion evaluation is subjective and has limited sensitivity, potentially leading to delayed or incorrect detection of treatment failure. To address this issue, the application of machine learning (ML) methods for smear conversion detection has gained attention for its potential to enhance precision and effectiveness.

The study [4] by W. Gichuhi, Mark Magumba, Manish Kumar, and Roy Mayega explores the use of machine learning models to identify individual risk factors for tuberculosis treatment non-adherence in Mukono district, Uganda. The study analyzed records of 838 TB patients from different health facilities and developed five machine learning algorithms. The best-performing model was Support Vector Machine (SVM) with an accuracy of 91.28%. Identified risk factors included TB type, GeneXpert results, ART status, sub-country, contacts below 5 years, and other demographic and clinical factors. The study highlights the potential of machine learning to differentiate adherent and non-adherent patients and suggests its use as a screening tool for targeted interventions. However, limitations in data capture and heterogeneous classifications were noted. Despite challenges, machine learning shows promise in improving TB management and decision-making in resource-constrained settings.

Another study by Swathi S. Kundaram, Ketki C. Pathak, A. D. Darji, Jignesh and N. Sarvaiya [7] focused on developing a computer-aided diagnosis (CAD) system for tuberculosis disease classification using two approaches. The first approach involved utilizing ANNs and SVMs, while the second approach employed a deep convolutional neural network (DCNN) with GPU-based Keras library and TensorFlow as a backend. Preprocessing techniques like grayscale, median filtering, and gamma correction were applied, along with methods like Otsu and Hough transform for segmentation and curve detection. For feature extraction, the gray level combination matrix was employed. The DCNN-based classification's accuracy was 99.24%, compared to the ANN-SVM-based classification's 94.6%. The authors claimed that while the DCNN strategy is better suited for bigger datasets, an ANN method is better suited for smaller datasets. The use of this CAD system may help in TB early diagnosis.

Image classification algorithms were also used to separate chest X-ray pictures with and without TB in a research by Mohammad Alsaffar in 2021 [8]. The KERAS framework and the RESNET50 neural network were used to extract features after the pictures had undergone preprocessing procedures including padding and scaling. In two classification situations, the SVM, the logistic regression, and the K-Nearest Neighbors (KNN) techniques were used, along with cross-validation and the creation of training and test sets. The findings showed an accuracy of more than 85%, with SVM doing the best. The work demonstrates the promise of image classification methods, in particular deep learning, for detecting TB using chest X-ray imaging.

Three convolutional neural networks (CNNs) were used in a 2019 study on the categorization of X-ray chest images by Ege Kesim, Tamer Olmez and Zumray Dokur [9]. Thirteen convolutional layers and two fully linked layers made up the first CNN (CNN-1), which was designed to test the effects of layer density on classification performance. Four convo-lution layers and two completely linked layers made up the second and third CNNs (CNN-2 and CNN-3), which examined how the size of an image affected categorization performance. The study findings indicated that increasing the number of layers did not enhance the network's generalization, and the classification performance remained unchanged for input images of size 128×128 or 256×256. However, the performance notably decreased for images smaller than 128×128. The overall goal of the study was to investigate if smaller network topologies may perform more effectively when classifying X-ray chest images. The study had an 86% success rate.

CheXNet, a 121-layer convolutional neural network (CNN) that was trained on chest X-ray for pneumonia identification, was introduced by Pranav Rajpurkar et al. in 2017 [10]. The network was optimized using dense connections and batch normalization and trained end-to-end using minibatches of size 16 with an initial learning rate of 0.001. Input images were downscaled to 224x224 and normalized based on the mean and standard deviation of images in the ImageNet training set. Random horizontal flipping was added to the training data. CheXNet achieved an F1 score of 0.435, which was found to be statistically significantly higher than the performance of radiologists. Furthermore, the team extended CheXNet to detect 14 diseases in ChestX-ray 14 and achieved state-of-the-art results for all 14 diseases. The network is capable of providing the probability of pneumonia and generating a heatmap highlighting the areas of the image most indicative of pneumonia.

3 The Methodology

The methodology section describes the strategy employed in this study to examine how machine learning techniques may be utilized to forecast smear conversion in tuberculosis (TB) patients. It offers a thorough explanation of the data utilized, including how it was gathered and prepared. In order to demonstrate the organization and logic of the research process, a conceptual map is shown. The section discusses feature extraction and the choice of machine learning models, placing special emphasis on the techniques and equipment used. The suggested model's validation process and performance assessment criteria are given to guarantee its dependability and correctness. This part creates a strong basis for the future analysis and discussion of the study findings by providing a clear and organized approach.

In terms of research methods, the medical field will be examined, with a special emphasis on machine learning. To gain valuable insights and guidance, a visit to the Welisara Chest Hospital in Ragama, Sri Lanka was made, where discussions were held with medical professionals, including the hospital director and chest physicians. These interactions helped identify gaps in the medical field that could be addressed through research. To narrow down the research topic, extensive reading of research papers suggested by the physician was conducted. After careful analysis, the prediction and analysis of smear conversion in tuberculosis patients emerged as the chosen topic due to its potential impact in the medical field and its relevance to addressing a critical issue faced by tuberculosis patients.

3.1 Ethical Clearance

Obtaining ethical approval is a crucial step in research involving human subjects. For this study, the necessary ethical approval was obtained from the Ethics Review Committee of the Ragama Medical Faculty, Sri Lanka, with the approval number [P/173/12/2022]. The process involved submitting a proposal along with various documents, including a patient information sheet (PIS), a questionnaire formulated with input from doctors and medical professionals, an informed consent form (ICF), and an application form. This approval signifies that the study was conducted with ethical considerations, prioritizing the well-being and safety of the participants. The Ethics Review Committee ensures compliance with ethical principles, such as obtaining informed consent, protecting privacy and confidentiality, and minimizing potential risks associated with the study.

3.2 Data Collection

The data collection process for this study involved gathering relevant information from tuberculosis (TB) patients at the Welisara Chest Hospital in Ragama. After obtaining ethical approval from the Ethics Review Committee, a patient information sheet (PIS) and a questionnaire were developed with the input of doctors and medical professionals. These instruments were used to collect data on patient demographics, medical history, and sputum smear results. Informed consent was obtained from each participant prior to data collection. The data collection process was conducted in a structured manner, ensuring confidentiality and privacy of the participants.

The study population for this research comprised pulmonary tuberculosis patients registered at the Welisara Chest Hospital in Sri Lanka from April 2022 to April 2023. Initially, a dataset of 288 patients was collected. However, during the data collection phase, it was identified that not all patients had accessible before-treatment chest X-ray images. As part of the planned image processing approach to identify tuberculosis using X-ray images, patients without available images were carefully evaluated and subsequently excluded from further analysis. This curation process resulted in a final dataset of 185 patients, ensuring the integrity and reliability of the subsequent analysis. The collected data will serve as the foundation for the evaluation and assessment of machine learning methods in predicting smear conversion in tuberculosis patients. A summary of the collected patient details can be found in Table 1.

Table 1. Overview of collected patient's details.

Smear Status	Number of patients before intensive phase	Number of patients after intensive phase
Positive	103	40
Negative	82	145
Total	185	185

3.3 Neural Network Design

After collecting the dataset of pulmonary tuberculosis (PTB) patients, the data was meticulously recorded in an Excel sheet, ensuring accuracy and attention to detail. In addition to the patient information, chest X-ray images underwent an image processing approach [11] to determine their positivity for tuberculosis. The results of the image analysis were then incorporated into the Excel sheet as a separate column, serving as an input variable for further analysis. The utilization of this combined dataset provides a comprehensive and reliable foundation for my research. To illustrate the methodology employed in this study, a flowchart (Fig. 1) has been designed, showcasing the step-by-step process from data collection to analysis.

Data Pre-processing. In the data preprocessing phase, the variables in the dataset were analyzed to understand their characteristics and suitability for the study. The output variable of interest was the smear status after the intensive phase of tuberculosis treatment. The input variables included demographic information and the results of X-ray images.

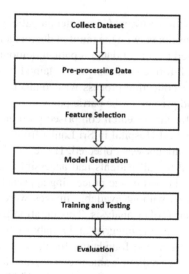

Fig. 1. Flow chat of the methodology

During this analysis, it was observed that the dataset exhibited an imbalance in the distribution of the output variable, with a significant majority of negative smear status cases compared to positive cases.

After the feature selection procedure, the Synthetic Minority Over-sampling Technique (SMOTE) was used to solve the problem of class imbalance. To balance the dataset, SMOTE creates artificial samples of the minority class (positive smear status). SMOTE was used to add more synthetic positive instances to the dataset, ensuring a more even representation of both positive and negative smear status.

Feature Selection. The factors that were most closely connected with the after treatments smear status following treatments were identified using a feature selection technique after the data had undergone preprocessing. The aim was to identify the subset of factors that significantly affect smear status prediction. These chosen variables were then used as input parameters for the subsequent modeling phases since they showed substantial correlations with the outcome variable.

ANN Modeling. An Artificial Neural Network (ANN) architecture was chosen due to its ability to identify intricate linkages and patterns in the data. The ANN model comprised an input layer, a hidden layer, and an output layer. The input layer had 8 nodes and employed the Rectified Linear Unit (ReLU) activation function, known for effectively handling non-linearities. The hidden layer consisted of 6 nodes, also using the ReLU activation function. The number of nodes in the hidden layer was determined through experimentation and hyperparameter tuning, striking a balance between model complexity and performance. The output layer had one node and utilized the sigmoid activation function, ideal for binary classification problems as it produces probability values between 0 and 1.

During model compilation, the Adam optimizer was employed, a popular adaptive learning rate optimization algorithm. This optimizer contributes to the model's efficiency during training. The binary cross-entropy loss function was selected as it suits binary classification tasks, especially when dealing with probabilistic output like sigmoid. Accuracy was chosen as the evaluation metric, measuring the proportion of correct predictions over the total number of samples.

Training and Evaluation. Using the pre-prepared training information together with the specified architectural framework, the model was trained. The training procedure required a predetermined number of iterations, or epochs, where each epoch represented a thorough examination of the training data. Backpropagation was used by the model during training to alter its internal parameters with the goal of minimizing the difference between projected outputs with the actual target values.

Following training, stratified K-fold cross-validation validation sets were used to assess the model's performance. By evaluating the model's performance across several validation sets while preserving the percentage of samples from each class, this strategy guaranteed the model's capacity to generalize. Evaluation measures, such accuracy, were calculated to assess how well the model predicted the smear state on unobserved data. Additionally, the training records were kept in order to examine the model's learning process and spot any problems like overfitting or underfitting. These histories tracked changes in loss and accuracy over the course of each epoch.

4   Results

The results of the methods used to predict smear conversion in TB patients using machine learning techniques are presented in this chapter. This chapter offers a thorough analysis of the findings, highlighting the effectiveness of the proposed model and the learnings from the research (Fig. 2).

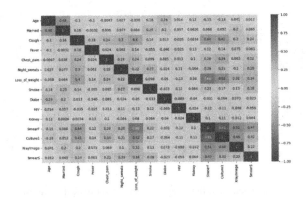

Fig. 2. Heatmap of correlation of variables

A detailed examination of the dataset was performed throughout the feature selection phase to discover factors that had strong correlations with the output variable, which represented the smear status following treatments. Age, gender, education level, marital status, the presence of symptoms like a fever, cough, chest pain, and night sweats, smoking habits, loss of weight, the presence of comorbidities like diabetes and HIV, kidney function, as well as the outcomes of smear microscopy and culture tests were some of the significant variables identified through this analysis. Individual graphs were created to show these variables' connections to the output variable in order to provide more in-depth insights. These graphs (Fig. 3) provided a visual picture of the relationships among each of the variables and the probability of smear conversion, allowing for a deeper comprehension of how those relationships affected the result.

Following a thorough investigation, it was possible to identify the importance of correlation among the parameters and the smear status following treatments, allowing the most important variables to be chosen for the model. These thoughtfully selected factors significantly increase the model's predictive power and accuracy, assuring its efficacy in correctly identifying and forecasting the smear status following treatments.

The existence of symptoms of coughing, chest discomfort, loss of weight, night sweats, smoking habits, the findings of smear microscopy and culture tests, and X-ray image analysis were among the chosen factors. These factors were deliberately chosen due to their high correlations with the smear status following therapy and their ability to offer insightful information for prognostication. To provide a statistical overview of the variables, the following figure (Fig. 4) will present relevant descriptive statistics and key characteristics of each variable, further supporting their relevance and importance in the subsequent modeling process.

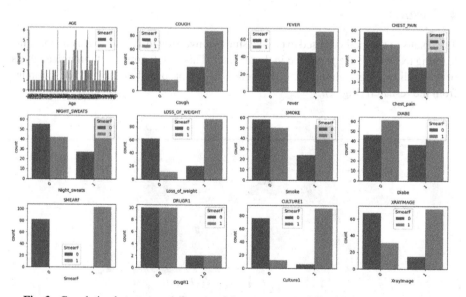

Fig. 3. Correlation between each factor and the smear status following the intense phase.

Then a neural network model was developed with specific parameters: an input layer with 8 nodes using the ReLU activation function, a hidden layer with 6 nodes also using ReLU activation, and an output layer with 1 node using the sigmoid activation function.

	Age	Cough	Fever	Chest_pain	Night_sweats	Loss_of_weight	Smoke	Diabe	SmearF	DrugR1	Culture1	XrayImage	SmearS
count	185.000000	185.000000	185.000000	185.000000	185.000000	185.000000	185.000000	185.000000	185.000000	24.000000	185.000000	185.00000	185.000000
mean	52.875676	0.659459	0.616216	0.437838	0.475676	0.605405	0.416216	0.421622	0.556757	0.166667	0.524324	0.47027	0.216216
std	16.064770	0.475177	0.487626	0.497467	0.500763	0.490000	0.494266	0.495159	0.498116	0.380693	0.500763	0.50047	0.412781
min	18.000000	0.000000	0.000000	0.000000	0.000000	0.000000	0.000000	0.000000	0.000000	0.000000	0.000000	0.00000	0.000000
25%	43.000000	0.000000	0.000000	0.000000	0.000000	0.000000	0.000000	0.000000	0.000000	0.000000	0.000000	0.00000	0.000000
50%	55.000000	1.000000	1.000000	0.000000	0.000000	1.000000	0.000000	0.000000	1.000000	0.000000	1.000000	0.00000	0.000000
75%	65.000000	1.000000	1.000000	1.000000	1.000000	1.000000	1.000000	1.000000	1.000000	0.000000	1.000000	1.00000	0.000000
max	80.000000	1.000000	1.000000	1.000000	1.000000	1.000000	1.000000	1.000000	1.000000	1.000000	1.000000	1.00000	1.000000

Fig. 4. Descriptive analysis of the variables

The model was compiled with the Adam optimizer, binary cross-entropy loss function, and accuracy as the evaluation metric. To ensure consistent settings for each run, the dataset was divided into 30% for testing and 70% for training.

On the training dataset, a 3-fold cross-validations with 400 epochs was carried out after creating a neural network model using the given parameters. The accompanying Fig. 5 displays accuracy and loss curves for every fold. Through this validation method, the model's effectiveness and robustness were evaluated.

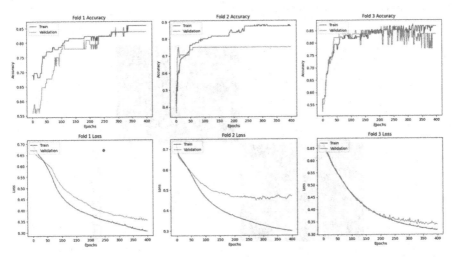

Fig. 5. Cross validation accuracy and loss plots, respectively

The model was also further assessed using the testing dataset. The accuracy as well as loss curves for the evaluation are shown below (Fig. 6). These curves include information about the model's results on both the training and testing datasets, enabling a thorough evaluation of how well it predicts the smear status after therapy.

The model's performance for forecasting the after-treatment smear status was highly effective, according to the model assessment findings. For class 0 (signifying a negative smear status), the F1-score, precision, and recall were 0.91, 0.95, and 0.87, respectively. Similar results were obtained for class 1 (indicating a positive smear status) with an F1-score, accuracy, and recall of 0.91, 0.87, and 0.95 respectively. These scores show that the model can categorize both positive and negative situations with accuracy. The

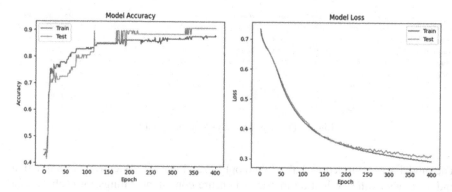

Fig. 6. Outcomes of the testing data's validation

model's total accuracy was 0.91, showing that it was successful in predicting the smear status following treatments. The model's performance is obviously displayed in (Fig. 7) below, further highlighting its accurate prediction skills. A heatmap was used to display the outcomes of the validation process.

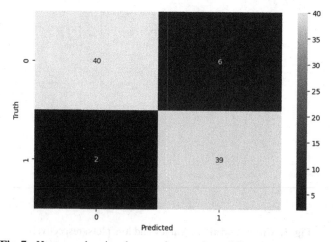

Fig. 7. Heatmap showing the neural network model's output outcomes.

The heatmap analysis showed areas of accurate and wrong classifications on the test set, giving a visual depiction of the model's predictions. This graphic provided insightful information about the model's general success in correctly predicting the after-treatment smear status. It included a thorough analysis of the model's predictive capabilities. A Comparative analysis of several research studies related to identification of TB with my suggested model can be found in Table 2.

Table 2. Comparison of several research studies and my proposed model

References	Year	Features of Dataset	Method	Accuracy
Haron et al. [4]	2022	838 patients	Random Forest	89.97%
			Linear Regression	88.30%
			ANN	88.30%
			SVM	91.28%
			AdaBoost	91.05%
M. Alsaffar et al. [8]	2021	138 Radiographs	SVM ResNet50	85.0%
			SVM KNN	
Lopes et al. [12]	2017	1120 Records	GoogleNet ResNet	84.7%
			VGGNet	
Proposed model	2023	185 Patients	Neural Network	90.80%

5 Discussion

The neural network model's predictions for the after-treatment smear status show how good it is at classifying data. The model performed well, as seen by its 90.80% total accuracy on the test set. The recall, precision, and F1-score metrics attained for both classes provide additional evidence for this accuracy.

The model's precision for class 0, which represents a negative smear status following treatments, was 95%, showing a low risk of false positives. The recall score of 87% indicates that a sizable number of true negative situations were effectively detected by the model. The balanced performance of the model in categorizing negative situations is supported by the F1-score of 91%. Likewise, the accuracy of the model for class 1, which represents a positive smear status following therapies, was 87%, demonstrating its capacity to recognize genuine positive instances. The recall value of 95% implies that the model successfully captured a majority of the positive cases. The F1-score of 91% highlights the model's effectiveness in correctly classifying positive cases.

The obtained results reflect the model's ability to accurately classify both positive and negative cases, contributing to its reliability in predicting the after treatments smear status. The heatmap analysis further supports the model's performance, visually displaying the areas of correct and incorrect classifications.

6 Conclusions

The developed neural network model showcases promising advancements in accurately predicting smear status after intensive phase of tuberculosis treatments in a medical context. The accuracy of 90.80% and balanced classification of positive and negative smear statuses position it as a valuable tool for enhancing clinical decision-making and patient care. The model's effectiveness is underpinned by meticulous data preprocessing and thoughtful feature selection, which contribute to its impressive predictive power. Rigorous validation using a 3-fold cross-validation approach further reinforces its efficacy, demonstrating robust performance with exceptional precision, recall, and

F1-scores for both classes. These compelling results instill confidence in the model's reliability and practical utility in real-world scenarios. To augment its generalizability, future validation on larger and diverse datasets is warranted, along with careful consideration of potential limitations like data availability and biases. Overall, this neural network model signifies a significant step forward in tuberculosis treatment management, with the potential to improve patient outcomes and drive advancements in public health efforts. Embracing data-driven technologies and continued research, this model holds the promise of becoming an indispensable asset for clinicians in their relentless fight against tuberculosis.

References

1. CDCTB: Tuberculosis (TB)-Basic TB Facts: Centers for Disease Control and Prevention, 19 June 2019. https://www.cdc.gov/tb/topic/basics/default.htm. Accessed 27 Nov 2022
2. "Fact Sheets | General | Tuberculosis: General Information | TB | CDC. 17 August 2022. https://www.cdc.gov/tb/publications/factsheets/general/tb.htm. Accessed 22 Jan 2023
3. Meshesha, M.D.: Predictors of sputum culture conversion time among MDR/RR TB patients on treatment in a low-income setting. PLoS ONE 17(11), e0277642 (2022). https://doi.org/10.1371/journal.pone.0277642
4. Gichuhi, H.W., Magumba, M., Kumar, M., Mayega, R.W.: A machine learning model to explore individual risk factors for tuberculosis treatment non-adherence in Mukono district. Health Inform. 21, 238 (2022). https://doi.org/10.1101/2022.12.01.22283003
5. Khan, M.T., Kaushik, A.C., Ji, L., Malik, S.I., Ali, S., Wei, D.-Q.: Artificial neural networks for prediction of tuberculosis disease. Front. Microbiol.Microbiol. 10, 395 (2019). https://doi.org/10.3389/fmicb.2019.00395
6. Mokti, K., et al.: Predictors of delayed sputum smear conversion among pulmonary tuberculosis patients in Kota Kinabalu, Malaysia: a retrospective cohort study. Medicine 100(31), e26841 (2021). https://doi.org/10.1097/MD.0000000000026841
7. AlvinoRock, C., BijolinEdwin, E., Arvinthan, C., Kevin JosephPaul, B., Jayaraj, R., JebaKumar, R.J.S.: Computer Aided Skin Disease (CASD) classification using machine learning techniques for iOS platform. In: Mehta, M., Fournier-Viger, P., Patel, M., Lin, J.C.-W. (eds.) Tracking and Preventing Diseases with Artificial Intelligence. ISRL, vol. 206, pp. 201–216. Springer, Cham (2022). https://doi.org/10.1007/978-3-030-76732-7_9
8. Alsaffar, M., et al.: Detection of tuberculosis disease using image processing technique. Mob. Inf. Syst. 2021, 1–7 (2021). https://doi.org/10.1155/2021/7424836
9. Kesim, E., Dokur, Z., Olmez, T.: X-ray chest image classification by a small-sized convolutional neural network. In: 2019 Scientific Meeting on Electrical-Electronics & Biomedical Engineering and Computer Science (EBBT), Istanbul, Turkey, pp. 1–5. IEEE (2019). https://doi.org/10.1109/EBBT.2019.8742050
10. Rajpurkar, P., et al.: CheXNet: Radiologist-Level Pneumonia Detection on Chest X-Rays with Deep Learning. arXiv, 25, December 2017. Accessed 23 Mar 2023. http://arxiv.org/abs/1711.05225
11. Sethy, P.K., Behera, S.K.: Detection of Coronavirus Disease (COVID-19) Based on Deep Features. ENGINEERING, March 2020. https://doi.org/10.20944/preprints202003.0300.v1
12. Lopes, U.K., Valiati, J.F.: Pre-trained convolutional neural networks as feature extractors for tuberculosis detection. Comput. Biol. Med.. Biol. Med. 89, 135–143 (2017). https://doi.org/10.1016/j.compbiomed.2017.08.001

Investigation on Cost-Sensitivity in EEG-Based Confusion Emotion Recognition Systems via Ensemble Learning

Dasuni Ganepola[1]([✉]), Indika Karunaratne[1], and M. W. P. Maduranga[2]

[1] University of Moratuwa, Moratuwa, Sri Lanka
dasuniganepola@gmail.com
[2] General Sir John Kotelawala Defence University, Dehiwala-Mount Lavinia, Sri Lanka

Abstract. Confusion is an important academic emotion that usually arises when a student cannot integrate new information with existing knowledge. Identifying confused students for an educator is a very challenging task as students may not express their confusion state. Recently, EEG – based confusion emotion recognition systems had been developed using machine learning as an aid for educators to help identify their confused learners easily. But the problem with those studies were that the systems were developed for experimental purposes and not for real world usage. Due to this, educators are not able to experience the benefits of such systems. In this study, we explored the possibility of developing a system fitting for a practical application using the concepts in cost sensitive machine learning. We developed two heterogenous machine learning models (Serial and Parallel combination) with the aim of achieving a tradeoff between prediction performance and cost sensitivity in terms of reduced misclassification cost. Results showed that the designed serial combination ensemble model achieved the best tradeoff between precision (highest value of 62.93%) and misclassification cost (lowest value of 1811.75) which could not be achieved by independent classifiers.

Keywords: Confusion Emotion Recognition · Cost Sensitivity · Ensemble Machine Learning · Tradeoff · Precision · Misclassification cost

1 Introduction

Cost sensitive machine learning is a subfield in Artificial Intelligence (AI) technology which is not relatively new but has gained popularity over the past few years to develop practical AI which can revolutionize our day to day lives [1, 2]. This subfield centers around three aspects:

- addressing problems associated with real-world data such as skewed class distributions and noise,
- efficient model training with minimal training costs,
- model generalizability – ability of the model to adapt to unseen real-world data [3].

D. Herath et al. (Eds.): APANConf 2023, CCIS 1995, pp. 39–50, 2024.
https://doi.org/10.1007/978-3-031-51135-6_4

This paper focuses on investigating and building cost sensitive confusion emotion recognition machine learning models that recognize the emotion from Electroencephalography (EEG) signals of learners. The authors envision building and deploying a real-world emotion recognition model that would revolutionize the domain of education through Emotion AI technologies. Previous research had been conducted to build confusion emotion recognition systems for learners. However, all works are accentuated in developing models that provided prediction accuracy in an experimental setup. None of the works researched on constructing models that would fit real-world applications.

This research would gap this problem and aims to build practical EEG-based emotion recognition systems that detect whether a learner is confused or not. The practicality of the model is defined as being efficient in terms of prediction accuracy and optimizing the cost of the model by minimizing the misclassification cost, thus creating a trade-off between the two interested parties. The authors designed a novel machine-learning framework using ensemble concepts. The main contribution of this paper is the novel ensemble approach utilized for serial ensemble combination.

This paper is organized as follows: Sect. 2 discusses the background of the research domain; Sect. 3 summarizes the study methodology; Sect. 4 presents the results; Sect. 5 provides a detailed discussion of the results followed by the conclusion.

2 Background

2.1 EEG -Based Confusion Emotion Recognition

Confusion emotion has been studied by educational psychologists who have suggested that confused learners are best identified by observing their verbal & behavioral cues [3] and through self-reporting. With cutting-edge technologies doorways opened for EEG-based confusion emotion recognition systems [5]. However, the biggest problem with Brain-Computer Interface (BCI) based emotion recognition systems is the high cost of building the system, which makes such systems impractical to use in the real world.

2.2 Previous Works on EEG-Based Confusion Emotion Recognition

Previous works were conducted to build such systems in an experimental environmental setting. All works focused on building models using various machine learning and deep learning classifiers, thereby comparing prediction accuracy to evaluate the best classifier. The most popular machine learning algorithms that were appreciated for high prediction accuracy were Support Vector Machine (SVM), k-Nearest Neighbor (kNN), Random Forest, XGBoost, and AdaBoost. The popular deep learning algorithms were Recurrent Neural Networks (RNN), Long-short term Memory (LSTM), and Bidirectional LSTM [4, 5].

All existing works relied on the same dataset as it is the only one with open access. However, the works had not scrutinized important concepts like dataset imbalance, the curse of dimensionality, bias-variance dilemma, model generalizability, etc., and has not focused on investigations to build cost-optimized high-performance systems that can be deployed in a real-world context.

3 Methodology

This research study aims on developing machine learning ensemble models aiming to build models having a tradeoff between prediction accuracy and cost sensitivity.

Research on cost-sensitive machine learning is not a novel concept as its research dates to the last decade. Previous research had shown that cost sensitivity can be achieved by developing algorithms specifically for cost learning which is rarely being done. The other method is filtering or combining prediction accuracies of several traditional machine learning algorithms which will account for misclassification costs to be considered. This technique is referred to as the ensemble approach. Learning involves combining multiple independent machine learning models (known as weak/base learners) into a single model. The decision of the prediction is taken collectively by the independent classifiers and finally averaged, weighted, or taken by the majority voting to predict the outcome.

This study will consider the construction of ensemble models to investigate if they can achieve a good trade-off between prediction accuracy and misclassification cost. The study followed a research approach which is described in the schematic diagram illustrated in Fig. 1.

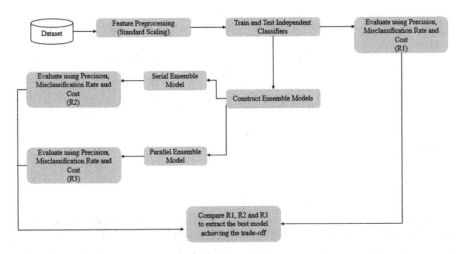

Fig. 1. Research Methodology of the Study

3.1 Data Set

The dataset used to train and test the ensemble models is from the work published by Wang et al. [5]. EEG signals from ten students watching MOOC videos in various science subjects were collected using single channel EEG headset and the signals were Fourier transformed to obtain Power Spectral Density values. The data set has 12811 data samples. For each data sample, there were PSD values for the following features: Theta/Alpha1, Alpha2/Theta, Beta2/(Alpha2+Theta), (Alpha2+Theta)/Beta2, Alpha2/Beta2, and Beta2/Alpha2 [5].

3.2 Design of Heterogenous Ensemble Model – Serial Combination

This design was inspired by the works of [6]. Their approach was improved in this study. Figure 4 shows how the combination of sub-classifiers in the heterogeneous ensemble is determined.

The foremost base classifier, named M_b was chosen having the highest variance. This indicated that the chosen classifier, M_i ($i - i^{th}$ sub classifier of the ensemble model) has the most overfitting property.

Next, pairwise disagreement between the $C_{i=0}$ model and the rest of the sub-classifiers is calculated. The pairwise disagreement measure which was proposed by Skalak [5] calculates the disagreements in the predictions between the base classifier and the classifier immediately combined with the former. This is done to portray ensemble diversity within the design model. Diversity among the sub-classifiers is regarded as a critical factor in ensemble model design. This is referred to as combining single classifiers that have different prediction accuracies and errors. It is because when combining single classifiers which make different kinds of errors, the overall prediction error can be reduced [5]. Assuming two classifiers as D_i & D_k, and N is the total number of samples, the relationship between the two classifiers is as follows (Table 1):

Table 1. Pairwise Disagreement Matrix

	D_k correct (1)	D_k incorrect (0)
D_i correct (1)	N^{11}	N^{10}
D_i incorrect (0)	N^{01}	N^{00}

The disagreement measure is calculated as follows:

$$Dis_{i,k} = \frac{N^0 + N^{10}}{N^{11} + N^{10} + N^{01} + N^{00}} \qquad (1)$$

The sub-classifier with the highest disagreement measure M_k (when compared to the base classifier M_b) is combined together by an ensemble voting mechanism. Accuracy A of the combined model ($A_{b,k}$) is evaluated against the accuracy of the base classifier (A_b). If $A_{b,k} > A_b$ the combined model is accepted and M_{i+1}.

Again, the pairwise disagreement is measured between the newly combined model and the rest of the classifiers. A classifier that has the highest disagreement measure is combined through the voting mechanism with the already combined model and prediction accuracy is evaluated. Finally, all sub-classifiers are combined to create the heterogenous ensemble model (Figs. 2 and 3).

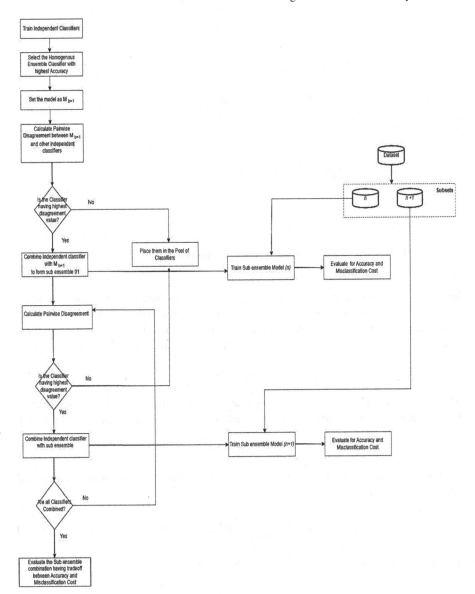

Fig. 2. Algorithm to develop heterogeneous ensemble model (serial combination)

3.2.1 Design of Heterogenous Ensemble Model - Parallel Combination

The authors adapted a Super Learner (SL) ensemble design for this approach. SLs are a type of stacking method where multiple classifiers which work on the same dataset are combined in layers. The stacking paradigm usually has two classifier layers: a set of base classifiers that are being trained in parallel and a meta-learner that will finally output the predictions by learning from a weighted prediction matrix created from predictions of the

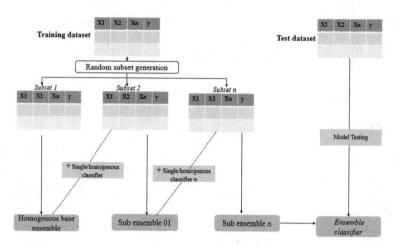

Fig. 3. Schematic diagram of heterogeneous ensemble model (serial combination)

base classifiers and the target variable. SLs are a special category of stacked ensembles where it can choose optimal learners from a group of base classifier candidates using cross-validation [6, 7]. Let ψ be the base classifier and j the number of base classifiers where j = 1 .. n. The prediction of a ψ_j trained and validated on a vth fold is defined as:

$$\Psi_{j(T,v)}(V(v)) \tag{2}$$

where (T, v) is the training dataset sample and (V, v), is the validation dataset sample. Let Z be the prediction matrix created by stacking the predictions of the base classifiers:

$$Z = \{\Psi_{j(T,v)}(V(v))\} \tag{3}$$

From the prediction matrix, the overall weight vector combination is calculated which is indexed by α:

$$m(z|\alpha) = \sum_{j=1}^{J} \alpha \Psi_{j(T,v)}(V(v)) \tag{4}$$

α' which defines the overall weight vector is defined as:

$$\alpha' = \arg min_{\alpha} \sum_{i=1}^{n} (Y_i - m(z_i|\alpha))^2 \tag{5}$$

Finally, the super learner model Ψs for a training data sample of T is created as. follows:

$$\Psi s(T) = \sum_{j=1}^{J} \alpha'_j \Psi_j(T) \tag{6}$$

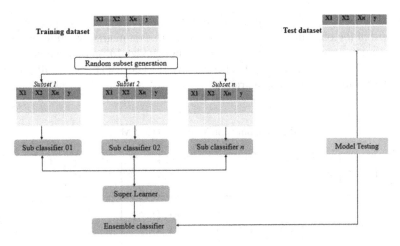

Fig. 4. Schematic diagram of heterogeneous ensemble model (parallel combination)

3.3 Algorithms Used for Ensemble Development

The algorithms used for developing the ensemble models are all supervised. A combination of both single classifiers and homogenous (bagging and boosting) is used. The algorithms selected for this study were the most frequently and most preferred ones from previous research works which had used the same data set. Accordingly, for single classifiers, support vector machines (SVM) and K nearest neighbors (kNN) were used. For homogenous (bagging): random forest (RFC) and Decision Tree classifier (DTC) were used. As for homogenous (boosting): AdaBoost (ADA) XGBoost (XG) and Cat-Boost (CAT) algorithms were utilized. All algorithms were hyperparameter-tuned using Evolutionary Algorithm.

3.4 Evaluation Metrics

The most common approach for creating classification algorithms is to reduce the likelihood of prediction error presuming that all errors cost equally. This is referred to as being cost–insensitive [1]. In reality, errors have different misclassification costs some errors are costlier than others. False Positive/Type I errors and False Negatives/Type II errors in binary classifications are considered the most costlier misclassification errors [8]. The following model error assessment measures were applied to compare the cost sensitivity of each ensemble model that was taken into consideration in this study:

1. *Confusion Matrix* – evaluates model's classification in terms of True Positive (TP), False Negative (FN), False Positive (FP), and True Negative (TN). The rate of each outcome is obtained by calculating its percentage over a total number of samples of the trained subsample.
2. *Precision* - Calculated as TP/(TP + FP). This measure shares an inverse relationship between itself and False Positive (FP) rate, i.e., if FP is equivalent to 0, the precision would be 100 [1].

3. *Cost Matrix* – an array of matrices derived from the confusion matrix which shows the cost of the outcomes for each cell in the confusion matrix. Multiplication of the two matrices provides the total cost for a certain model. Misclassification cost is the sum of False Negative (FN) and False Positive (FP) costs [1]. Table 2 illustrates the standard confusion and cost matrices.

Table 2. Confusion Matrix and Cost Matrix

Confusion Matrix	PREDICTED CLASS			Cost Matrix	PREDICTED CLASS		
ACTUAL CLASS		+	-	ACTUAL CLASS	C(i|j)	+	-
	+	TP	FP		+	-1	100
	-	FN	TN		-	1	0

where, TP is True Negative, FN – False Negative, FP – False Positive, TN is True Negative, and C(i|j) is the misclassification cost of class j as an example of class i.

4   Results and Interpretation

Table 3 illustrates the evaluation metric results obtained for single and homogenous classifiers.

Table 3. Evaluation Metric results for single and homogenous classifiers

Model	TP Rate	FP Rate	FN Rate	TN Rate	MC Rate	MC Cost	Precision
SVM	29.52	18.93	22.19	29.34	41.12	1915.19	60.92
KNN	48.46	0	51.53	0	51.53	51.33	100
RFC	0.01	47.37	1.30	50.23	48.61	4738.30	94.75
DTC	23.57	24.88	9.78	41.75	44.66	2497.78	48.64
CAT	26.84	21.61	20.60	30.93	42.21	2186.60	55.39
ADA	38.57	34.88	9.78	41.75	44.66	3497.78	52.51
XG	34.13	34.33	13.24	38.29	37.57	3446.24	522.62

Decision Tree Classifier (DTC) was not considered as it had the lowest precision and highest misclassification cost.

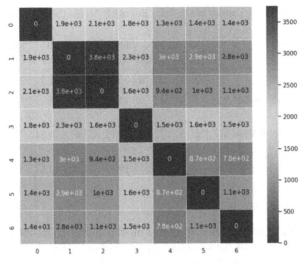

Fig. 5. Pairwise disagreement matrix of independent classifiers

To create the heterogenous ensemble in serial combination, sub-ensemble models were created by combining individual classifiers based on the pairwise disagreement measure (Fig. 5).

Where, 0 represents SVM, 1 – RFC, 2 – kNN, 3 – CAT, 4-ADA, 5 – XG, 6 -DTC.

Random Forest classifier was the homogenous classifier which produced the highest precision value (94.75%). Hence, this was chosen as the base classifier. A pairwise disagreement measure was calculated and accordingly, the highest pairwise disagreement measure obtained for random forest classifier was kNN (3.8e+0.3). The two classifiers were combined through the soft voting mechanism. The sub ensembles 2, 3, and 4 (S_En_2, S_En_3 and S_En_4) were created accordingly. Figure 6 shows the summary of the sub-ensemble creation (Table 4).

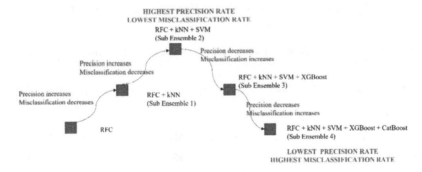

Fig. 6. Sub ensembles created by combining independent classifiers serially.

Table 4. Evaluation metrics of the Sub - Ensemble Model (Serial Combination)

Model	Classifiers	TP Rate	FP Rate	FN Rate	TN Rate	MC Rate	MC Cost	Precision
S_En_1	RFC+kNN	26.71	21.74	20.03	31.50	41.77	2194.03	55.12
Ensemble 2	RFC+kNN+SVM	30.49	17.96	15.75	35.77	33.71	1811.75	62.93
Ensemble 3	RFC+kNN+SVM+XG	25.57	22.89	17.92	33.61	40.81	2579.89	52.76
Ensemble 4	RFC+kNN+SVM+CAT	16.90	31.55	10.32	41.20	41.87	3165.32	34.88

As for the parallel combination ensemble model, all the independent classifiers utilized during the creation of the serial combination ensemble were used. The Logistic Regression algorithm was used as the standard meta-learner of the ensemble. Figure 8 illustrates the constructed heterogeneous parallel combination model (Fig. 7).

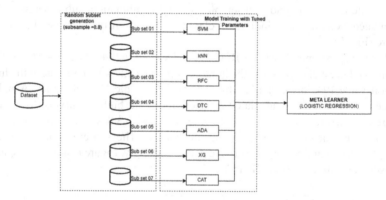

Fig. 7. Heterogenous Parallel Combination Ensemble model

The results of the evaluation metrics for the above model are illustrated in Table 5.

Table 5. Results of the Evaluation metrics of the Heterogenous Ensemble Model (Parallel Combination)

TP Rate	FP Rate	FN Rate	TN Rate	MC Rate	MC Cost	Precision
25.53	25.89	19.92	33.61	45.81	2608.92	50.63

5 Discussion

The results showed that even though precision was considerably higher for independent classifiers, the misclassification rate is also high, which accounts for the high misclassification cost.

The ensemble models created on the other hand did not overperform the precision metric when compared with the independent classifiers but the ensembles had reduced misclassification rates more than the independent classifiers accounting for reduced misclassification costs, thus creating a trade-off between prediction accuracy and misclassification cost.

When comparing the created sub-ensembles, it was observed that precision increased while misclassification cost decreased until the creation of the second sub-ensemble. However, combining independent classifiers with the second ensemble to create the third sub-ensemble led to a decrease in precision and an increase in misclassification. This was observed when combining the 4th and 5th sub ensembles subsequently. Therefore, the second sub-ensemble which is illustrated in Fig. 8 was chosen as the final ensemble model that produces the best tradeoff between precision (highest value of 62.93%) and misclassification cost (lowest value of 1811.75).

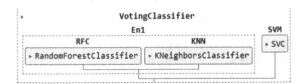

Fig. 8. Final Heterogenous Serial Combination Ensemble Model

6 Conclusion

This study investigates the cost sensitivity of confusion emotion classifiers developed from traditional supervised machine algorithms. The main aim of this research is to create a tradeoff between prediction accuracy and misclassification. The model's prediction accuracy and misclassification cost must be at its optimal level (not highest or lowest respectively) in order to achieve this trade-off. We attempted to create this tradeoff by designing a heterogenous ensemble model where the most frequently used independent machine learning algorithms for confusion emotion recognition in literature were combined to form a single model. Single classifiers: Support Vector Machine (SVM), k Nearest Neighbors (kNN), and homogenous ensemble algorithms: Random Forest (RF), XG Boost, Ada Boost, and the most recently developed Cat Boost algorithm were taken into consideration. During the experiment, the misclassification rate for the independent classifiers was calculated along with their prediction accuracy from the evaluation metric precision. It was observed that although the prediction accuracy is high, the misclassification rate is also high which accounts for increased misclassification costs. To solve this issue, an ensemble model was developed. The ensemble model that achieved the desired tradeoff had the classifiers integrated in a serial combination. The approach followed for this combination marks a novel methodology for confusion emotion classifier development. Results showed that the combination of RF, kNN and SVM generated the tradeoff between prediction accuracy and misclassification cost. The authors intend to expand this study by further increasing precision and lowering misclassification cost of EEG – based confusion emotion recognition systems.

References

1. Krishnapuram, B., Yu, S., Rao, B.: Cost-Sensitive Machine Learning. CRC Press, Boca Raton (2012)
2. Mienye, I.D., Sun, Y.: Performance analysis of cost-sensitive learning methods with application to imbalanced medical data. Inform. Med. Unlocked **25**, 100690 (2021). https://doi.org/10.1016/j.imu.2021.100690
3. Narassiguin, A.: Ensemble learning, comparative analysis and further improvements with dynamic ensemble selection. Artificial Intelligence [cs.AI]. Université de Lyon (2018). English. ffNNT: 2018LYSE1075ff. fftel-02146962f
4. Lodge, J.M., et al.: Understanding difficulties and resulting confusion in learning: an integrative review. Front. Educ. **3** (2018). https://doi.org/10.3389/feduc.2018.00049
5. Dong, S.-Q., et al.: How to improve machine learning models for lithofacies identification by practical and novel ensemble strategy and principles. Pet. Sci. **20**(2), 733–752 (2023)
6. Ganepola, D.: Assessment of learner emotions in online learning via educational process mining. In: 2022 IEEE Frontiers in Education Conference (FIE), Uppsala, Sweden, pp. 1–3 (2022). https://doi.org/10.1109/FIE56618.2022.9962490
7. Ganepola, D., Maduranga, M., Karunaratne, I.: Comparison of machine learning optimization techniques for EEG-based confusion emotion recognition. In: 2023 IEEE 17th International Conference on Industrial and Information Systems (ICIIS), Peradeniya, Sri Lanka, pp. 341–346 (2023). https://doi.org/10.1109/ICIIS58898.2023.10253515
8. Van der Laan, M.J., Polley, E.C., Hubbard, A.E.: Super learner. Stat. Appl. Genet. Mol. Biol. **6**(1) (2007). https://doi.org/10.2202/1544-6115.1309

Terminal Voltage Prediction of Solar-Wind Hybrid Systems with Time Series Decomposition: An Analysis and Comparative Study

Y. S. P. Weerasinghe[1]([✉]) [iD], H. K. I. S. Lakmal[2] [iD], D. R. Samila K. Wimalarathna[1] [iD], A. A. S. P. Jayasinghe[1] [iD], and A. R. C. Salgado[1] [iD]

[1] National Engineering Research and Development Center, Ja-Ela, Sri Lanka
{praveen,samila,shantha,salgado}@nerdc.lk
[2] Department of Mechatronic and Industry Engineering, NSBM Green University, Homagama, Sri Lanka
isuru.l@nsbm.ac.lk

Abstract. The demand for clean and sustainable energy sources has escalated in recent years due to growing concerns about climate change and the depletion of traditional fossil fuel reserves. Renewable energy technologies, such as wind and solar power, have emerged as promising alternatives to mitigate environmental impacts and ensure long-term energy security. The integration of solar and wind energy sources in hybrid renewable energy systems presents unique challenges due to the intermittent and variable nature of these sources. Accurate prediction of voltages in solar-wind hybrid systems is crucial for efficient power management and grid integration. Time series decomposition is a useful technique for analyzing and forecasting time series data, including solar and wind hybrid power generation. It involves breaking down the data into its constituent components, such as trend, seasonality, and residual, to gain insights and make predictions. This research paper aims to develop and compare time series decomposition prediction models for solar-wind hybrid voltages. The study investigates different decomposition methods, forecasting algorithms, and performance evaluation metrics to identify the most effective model for voltage prediction in hybrid renewable energy systems. Also shows the effectiveness of decomposition on prediction.

Keywords: Renewable energy · Time series decomposition · Hybrid power

1 Introduction

Voltage prediction plays a crucial role in power system operation and planning [1]. Accurate voltage forecasting allows power system operators to maintain grid stability, optimize dispatch, and make informed decisions for system maintenance and expansion. Various time-series forecasting methods are employed to predict voltage in hybrid solar wind systems. These include statistical methods like autoregressive integrated moving

D. Herath et al. (Eds.): APANConf 2023, CCIS 1995, pp. 51–62, 2024.
https://doi.org/10.1007/978-3-031-51135-6_5

average (ARIMA) [2], exponential smoothing (ETS) [3], and seasonal decomposition of time series (STL) [4]. Additionally, machine learning techniques such as artificial neural networks (ANNs), support vector regression (SVR) [5], and long short-term memory (LSTM) [6] networks are also widely used. On top of these techniques, the data series can be decomposed and train forecasting models on the decomposed components separately. One advantage of training forecasting models after decomposing the time series is the ability to capture different components or patterns within the data. By decomposing the series into its constituent parts, such as trend, seasonality, and residual components, it becomes easier to model and predict each component separately. This allows for more accurate and reliable predictions, as the models can capture and account for the unique characteristics of each component. Furthermore, decomposing the time series can provide insights into the underlying dynamics of the system and help identify any anomalous patterns or behaviors that may impact voltage levels.

The research aims to evaluate the advantages of training forecasting models with time series decomposition methods. The research involves collecting historical voltage data from solar-wind hybrid systems and analyzing the patterns and characteristics of voltage fluctuations.

2 Literature Review

Accurate voltage prediction is essential for the efficient operation and control of solar and wind hybrid systems. Solar and wind energy generation fluctuates due to weather conditions, making it challenging to accurately predict the power output and voltage levels. The variability and uncertainty of renewable energy sources introduce challenges in voltage prediction [7]. Hybrid systems often combine solar and wind energy sources, which further complicates voltage prediction. The integration of multiple sources with different characteristics requires advanced modelling techniques to account for their combined effects on the voltage levels [8]. Hybrid systems must be connected to the electrical grid, which introduces challenges related to power quality and stability. Voltage fluctuations caused by intermittent renewable energy sources can impact the stability and reliability of the grid, requiring accurate voltage prediction to ensure proper grid integration [9]. Accurate voltage prediction often relies on historical data for modelling and forecasting. However, in some cases, there may be limited historical data available for hybrid systems, especially in emerging or rapidly expanding renewable energy markets. This scarcity of data can pose challenges in developing accurate voltage prediction models [10]. Hybrid renewable energy systems involve complex interactions between various components, including solar panels, wind turbines, energy storage systems, and control devices. Modelling and predicting voltage levels in such complex systems require an accurate representation of system dynamics and their interdependencies [11].

2.1 Existing Time Series Forecasting Approaches

There are several existing time series forecasting approaches that can be applied to various domains. Autoregressive Integrated Moving Average (ARIMA) is a widely used approach for time series forecasting, particularly for stationary data. It combines autoregressive (AR), differencing (I), and moving average (MA) components to model and predict future values based on past observations [12]. Exponential smoothing methods, such as Single Exponential Smoothing (SES), Double Exponential Smoothing (DES), and Triple Exponential Smoothing (TES) or Holt-Winters method, are effective for forecasting time series data with trends and seasonal patterns [13]. Seasonal Autoregressive Integrated Moving Average (SARIMA) is an extension of the ARIMA model that incorporates seasonal components. It captures both the autoregressive and moving average effects along with seasonal differencing to handle seasonal time series data [14]. Vector Autoregression (VAR) is a multivariate time series forecasting method that models the dependencies among multiple variables by considering their lagged values. It is suitable for capturing the dynamics and interrelationships between variables [15].

Long Short-Term Memory (LSTM) Neural Networks are a type of recurrent neural network (RNN) that is effective for modelling and forecasting sequential data. It can capture long-term dependencies and has been successfully applied to time series forecasting tasks [6]. Prophet is a forecasting library developed by Facebook that combines additive and multiplicative time series components with seasonality, holidays, and trend flexibility. It is designed for forecasting time series with various patterns and has gained popularity for its simplicity and effectiveness [16]. Voltage forecasting method based on the seasonal decomposition of time series (STL) and neural networks. They demonstrate that time series decomposition can effectively decompose the voltage data into trend, seasonal, and residual components, enabling accurate prediction [17].

Time series forecasting techniques that are frequently utilized for a variety of data sources include ARIMA, exponential smoothing, SARIMA, VAR, LSTM, and Prophet. In order to build voltage prediction models for hybrid solar-wind systems, time series decomposition techniques need to be explored more thoroughly. SARIMA and LSTM are suitable for long-term forecasting, whereas AR models are suitable for short-term forecasting based on temporal relationships. This study uses data series STL decomposition techniques to create a voltage prediction model for solar-wind hybrid systems.

3 Methodology

3.1 Data Collection and Preprocessing

The data-gathering arrangement for solar and wind voltages is depicted in Fig. 1. The Solar-Wind Hybrid controller using pulse width modulation (PWM) seamlessly switches between solar and wind power based on availability. A battery with a maximum voltage of 48 V is connected as the primary power source for the light load. As backup sources for charging the battery, solar and wind energy are utilized. The maximum voltage necessary to switch between solar and wind power is determined by the charge controller. The setups use an 80 W solar panel and a 100 W Savonius vertical axis wind turbine (VAWT) for solar and wind power generation, respectively. The data is logged onto controller monitoring software every second. However, the logged data was converted to hourly data before the analysis. Variations of terminal voltages of the solar system and the wind system are displayed in Fig. 2 and Fig. 3 respectively. For a month-long period, detailed data was meticulously recorded at regular intervals of every second. Throughout this time frame, a continuous stream of observations was diligently captured.

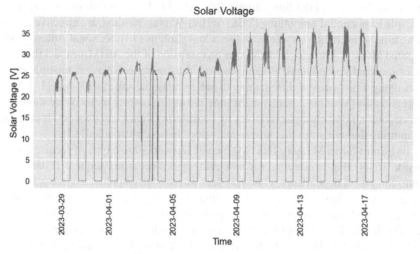

Fig. 1. Solar Wind Hybrid Setup

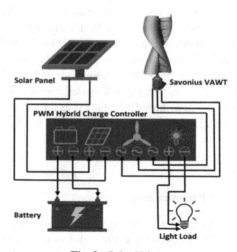

Fig. 2. Solar Voltage

3.2 Forecasting Model and the Time Series Decomposition Technique

Forecasting Model: The autoregressive (AR) forecasting model is a widely used approach for time series forecasting [18]. The AR model predicts future values based on a linear combination of past observations. In the AR model, the predicted value at a given time step is a weighted sum of the previous values in the time series. The weights

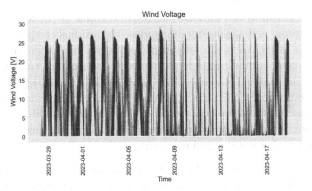

Fig. 3. Wind Voltage

or coefficients are determined through the autoregressive component of the model. The autoregressive component considers the relationship between the current observation and the previous observations at different lags. The order of the AR model specifies the number of previous observations included in the model. Throughout our experiment data from the past two days was used to predict the voltage of the terminal. The order of our models is 48, which represents the data from the previous two days, because we are using hourly data for our research. The AR model assumes that the future value of a time series variable is a linear combination of its past values, with an added error term to account for random fluctuations or noise. Mathematically, an AR(p) model of order p can be represented as follows:

$$y(t) = c + \Sigma(\varphi i * y(t - i)) + \varepsilon(t) \tag{1}$$

where, $y(t)$ is the value of the time series variable at time t. c is a constant term (the intercept of the model). φi (phi) represents the coefficients of the past values of the variable, from $i = 1$ to $i = p$. $y(t - i)$ denotes the past values of the variable at time t $- i$ (i.e., lagged values). $\varepsilon(t)$ is the error term at time t, which represents the difference between the predicted value and the actual value at time t. The order of the AR model, denoted by 'p', represents the number of lagged values used to predict the current value. For instance, an AR(1) model uses only the immediate past value to make predictions, while an AR(2) model uses the two most recent past values.

Time Series Decomposition Techniques: When the AR model was developed, the time series data (i.e. terminal voltages) were decomposed into its constituent components, such as trend, seasonality, and residual, to better understand and analyze the underlying patterns. Seasonal Decomposition of Time Series (STL) is a popular decomposition method that decomposes a time series into three components: trend, seasonality, and residual [19]. The trend component captures the long-term behavior or the overall direction of the time series. It represents the underlying smooth and gradual changes in the data, removing the shorter-term fluctuations. The trend component helps identify any increasing or decreasing patterns over time. The seasonal component captures the recurring patterns or cycles within the data. It represents the regular and predictable fluctuations that occur at fixed intervals, such as daily, weekly, or yearly patterns. The seasonal component allows for the identification of seasonal effects and the understanding of their contribution to the overall time series. The residual component, also known as the remainder or the irregular component, represents the random and unexplained fluctuations in the data that cannot be attributed to the trend or seasonal patterns. It includes any noise, outliers, or unexpected variations that are not captured by the trend and seasonal components. STL is widely used because it can handle different types of seasonal patterns, is robust against outliers, and provides flexibility through control parameters. It enables a deeper understanding of the underlying patterns in time series data, facilitating further analysis and forecasting.

In the context of time series analysis for solar and wind terminal voltages, the terms "trend," "seasonal," and "residual" refer to the different components that make up the overall behavior of the time series data. These components are often obtained through time series decomposition techniques, which aim to break down the data into its fundamental constituents to better understand the underlying patterns and variations. The trend component represents the long-term movement or direction of the time series data. It shows the overall pattern or tendency of the voltage values to increase, decrease, or remain relatively constant over an extended period. In the context of solar and wind terminal voltages, the trend component might indicate the overall increasing or decreasing trend in voltage levels due to factors such as changing weather patterns, improvements in renewable energy infrastructure.

The seasonal component captures repetitive and predictable patterns that occur at fixed intervals or over specific periods, often referred to as seasons. For solar and wind terminal voltages, this component might indicate periodic variations in voltage levels that follow a regular pattern. For example, if there are daily or weekly variations due to the day-night cycle or weather patterns, the seasonal component would reflect these recurring fluctuations. The residual component, also known as the error component, represents the random fluctuations or noise left after removing the trend and seasonal components from the original time series data. It includes any unpredictable elements or short-term irregularities in the voltage values that cannot be attributed to the trend or seasonal patterns. These residuals might arise from measurement errors, temporary disturbances, or other unforeseen factors affecting the voltage levels.

Figure 4 and Fig. 5, as mentioned in your context, likely display these different components for both solar and wind terminal voltages. By examining these figures, researchers or analysts can visually assess how much of the variation in voltage is explained by the trend, seasonal patterns, and the unexplained residual fluctuations. Understanding these components can help in making informed decisions, forecasting future voltage behavior, identifying anomalies or irregularities, and designing strategies to optimize the operation and utilization of solar and wind energy systems.

3.3 Training

For model training and evaluation, the dataset is split into two parts: a training set and a testing (or validation) set. The training set is used to build the AR model by fitting it to the historical data. In this case, 70% of the available data is allocated to the training set, and the remaining 30% is used as the testing set. The training-test split helps in assessing

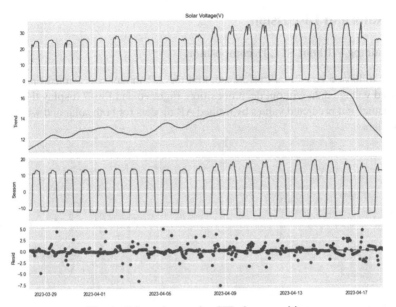

Fig. 4. Solar voltage using STL decomposition

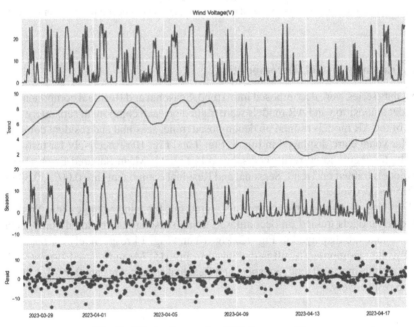

Fig. 5. Wind voltage using STL decomposition.

the model's performance on unseen data, providing an estimate of how well the model can generalize to make predictions beyond the training period.

4 Results and Discussion

4.1 Training Without STL Decomposition

In order to have a benchmark reference, first the AR model was trained on both solar and wind voltage data without decomposition. Figure 6 and Fig. 7 display the variation of the actual and predicted values by trained AR models for both solar and wind voltage testing data.

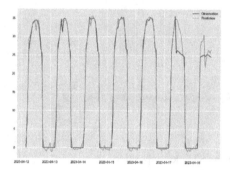 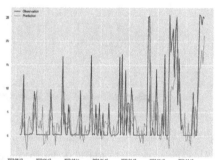

Fig. 6. Solar voltage prediction of the AR model without decomposition for test data

Fig. 7. Wind voltage prediction by the AR model without decomposition for test data

4.2 Training with STL Decomposition

Next, data series were decomposed into Trend, Seasonal and Residual components using STL decomposition and AR models were trained on each component separately. Predictions of the AR models trained on decomposed trend, seasonal and residual components of solar voltage are displayed in Fig. 8, Fig. 9 and Fig. 10 respectively for testing data. Finally, the recomposed result is displayed in Fig. 11. Mean Squared Error, (MSE) of AR models trained on Trend, Seasonal and Residual components are 0.0023, 0.3349 and 0.8915 respectively.

Similarly, the same process was also aired out for wind voltage data. Predictions of the AR models trained on decomposed trend, seasonal and residual components of wind voltage are displayed in Fig. 12, Fig. 13 and Fig. 14 respectively for testing data. Finally, the recomposed result is displayed in Fig. 15. Mean Squared Error (MSE) of AR models trained on Trend, Seasonal and Residual components are 0.0074, 1.1073 and 3.0605 respectively.

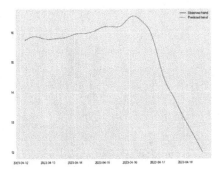

Fig. 8. AR model for trend

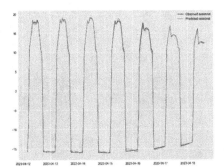

Fig. 9. AR model for seasonal

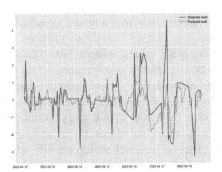

Fig. 10. AR model for residual

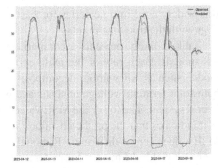

Fig. 11. Recompose results for Solar voltages

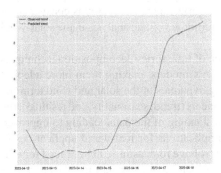

Fig. 12. AR model trend for wind

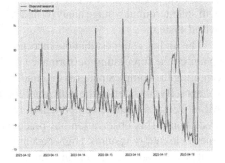

Fig. 13. AR model seasonal for wind

4.3 Comparative Analysis

The accuracy of the autoregressive (AR) models was assessed using a common evaluation metric called the Mean Squared Error (MSE). The MSE is a measure of the average squared difference between the predicted values and the actual (ground truth) values.

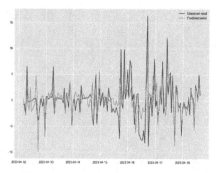 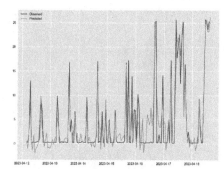

Fig. 14. AR model residual for wind   **Fig. 15.** Recompose results for wind voltages

It is widely used in time series forecasting to quantify how well a model's predictions align with the true data points.

Table 1 likely presents a comparison of the MSE values obtained from different AR models. Each row of the table corresponds to a specific configuration of the AR model, such as AR without decomposition and AR with time series decomposition for both solar terminal voltage analysis and wind terminal voltage analysis in a solar-wind hybrid system. The lower the MSE value, the better the model's predictive performance, as it indicates that the predicted values are closer to the actual values. By comparing the MSE values across different AR model configurations, researchers can identify which approach yields the most accurate forecasts for the hybrid renewable energy system being studied. According to the results presented in Table 1, it becomes evident that when AR models are trained with time series decomposition (i.e., using decomposed components like trend, seasonality, and residual), they exhibit higher accuracy compared to AR models trained without decomposition. This improvement in accuracy is consistent for both solar terminal voltage analysis and wind terminal voltage analysis in the solar-wind hybrid system.

The findings suggest that the incorporation of time series decomposition techniques enhances the forecasting performance of the AR models, making them more adept at capturing the complex patterns and underlying dynamics of the solar and wind terminal voltages. By considering the individual components (trend, seasonality, and residual), the AR model gains a more comprehensive understanding of the data, leading to improved predictions. This observation has practical implications for real-world applications in renewable energy systems. Higher accuracy in voltage forecasting can be crucial for efficient power management and grid integration, which can further optimize the utilization of solar and wind energy resources and enhance the overall stability and effectiveness of the hybrid renewable energy system.

Table 1. MSE Comparison

	Evaluation Metric	Without Decomposition	With Decomposition
Solar voltage analysis	MSE	1.97535	0.91225
	Hit Rate	81.05%	86.32%
Wind voltage analysis	MSE	5.96297	2.7724348
	Hit Rate	28.39%	50.97%

5   Conclusion

This research paper aims to enhance voltage forecasting in hybrid renewable energy systems by developing and comparing time series decomposition prediction models for solar-wind hybrid voltages. Through this study, valuable insights are gained into the application of time series decomposition techniques, allowing for the identification of the most effective model for accurate voltage prediction.

The findings of this research have the potential to offer significant benefits to system operators, energy planners, and researchers involved in optimizing power management and grid integration within solar-wind hybrid setups. By enhancing the stability and efficiency of renewable energy systems, these insights can contribute to the sustainable advancement of renewable energy technologies. In determining whether to employ AR models with or without decomposition, the research underscores the importance of considering the data's characteristics and the specific requirements of the forecasting task. Time series decomposition techniques are highlighted as valuable tools, enabling a deeper understanding of data dynamics, leading to improved forecasting accuracy and more informed decision-making processes.

Overall, this research contributes valuable knowledge to the field of renewable energy forecasting and underscores the benefits of utilizing time series decomposition methods in enhancing the performance and effectiveness of voltage prediction models in hybrid renewable energy systems.

References

1. Gómez-Pau, Á., Riba, J.R., Moreno-Eguilaz, M.: Time series RUL estimation of medium voltage connectors to ease predictive maintenance plans. Appl. Sci. **10**(24), 9041 (2020)
2. Box, G.E., Jenkins, G.M., Reinsel, G.C., Ljung, G.M.: Time Series Analysis: Forecasting and Control. Wiley, Hoboken (2015)
3. Jain, G., Mallick, B.: A study of time series models ARIMA and ETS (2017). SSRN 2898968
4. Cleveland, R.B., Cleveland, W.S., McRae, J.E., Terpenning, I.: STL: a seasonal-trend decomposition. J. Off. Stat. **6**(1), 3–73 (1990)
5. Sharifzadeh, M., Sikinioti-Lock, A., Shah, N.: Machine-learning methods for integrated renewable power generation: a comparative study of artificial neural networks, support vector regression, and Gaussian process regression. Renew. Sustain. Energy Rev. **108**, 513–538 (2019)
6. Hochreiter, S., Schmidhuber, J.: Long short-term memory. Neural Comput. **9**(8), 1735–1780 (1997)

7. Liu, Y., Kang, C., Wang, J., Shahidehpour, M.: Solar and wind power generation forecasting methods: a review. Energies **12**(10) (2019). https://doi.org/10.3390/en12101939
8. Pandžić, H., Filipović-Grčić, B.: Voltage stability assessment in power systems with high penetration of renewable energy sources: a review. Energies **11**(12), 3399. https://doi.org/10.3390/en11123399
9. Abo-Sinna, M.A., Abdel-Moneim, A.I.: Voltage and reactive power control techniques in distribution networks with renewable energy sources: a review. Energies **11**(4), 866. https://doi.org/10.3390/en11040866
10. Mohammadi-Ivatloo, B., Rabiee, A., Asadi, S., Hoseinzadeh-Beheshti, M.: Short-term load forecasting of microgrids using artificial neural networks: a case study of Borujerd county. Energies **7**(12), 8484–8500. https://doi.org/10.3390/en7128484
11. Silva, P., Rosas, F., Ramos, C., Soares, F., Gomes, Á., Seca, L.: Modeling and control of a wind-PV hybrid power system for hydrogen production. Energies **10**(4), 541. https://doi.org/10.3390/en10040541
12. Box, G.E., Jenkins, G.M., Reinsel, G.C.: Time Series Analysis: Forecasting and Control. Wiley, Hoboken
13. Hyndman, R.J., Athanasopoulos, G.: Forecasting: Principles and Practice. OTexts
14. Brockwell, P.J., Davis, R.A.: Introduction to Time Series and Forecasting, 3rd edn. Springer, Cham (2016). https://doi.org/10.1007/978-3-319-29854-2
15. Lütkepohl, H.: New Introduction to Multiple Time Series Analysis. Springer, Heidelberg (2005). https://doi.org/10.1007/978-3-540-27752-1
16. Taylor, S.J., Letham, B.: Forecasting at scale. Am. Stat. **72**(1), 37–45 (2018)
17. Wu, C.F., Guo, Y.B., Wang, X.Y., Liu, X.X.: Voltage forecasting based on seasonal decomposition of time series and neural network. Int. J. Electr. Power Energy Syst. **83**, 315–323 (2016)
18. Box, G.E., Jenkins, G.M., Reinsel, G.C., Ljung, G.M.: Time Series Analysis: Forecasting and Control. Wiley, Hoboken
19. Cleveland, R.B., Cleveland, W.S., McRae, J.E., Terpenning, I.J.: STL: a seasonal-trend decomposition procedure based on loess. J. Off. Stat. **6**(1), 3–73 (1990)
20. James, G., Witten, D., Hastie, T., Tibshirani, R.: An Introduction to Statistical Learning: with Applications in R. Springer, New York (2013). https://doi.org/10.1007/978-1-4614-7138-7

Early Prediction of Coronary Heart Disease Using Hybrid Machine Learning Models

Saraf Anika$^{(\boxtimes)}$ ⓘ, Mahmudul Islam, and Aditya Palit

East Delta University, Abdullah Al Noman Road, Noman Society, East Nasirabad, Khulshi, Chattogram 4209, Bangladesh
saraf.a@eastdelta.edu.bd

Abstract. Millions of people die each year from cardiovascular disease, which is the leading cause of death worldwide. Coronary Heart Disease is primarily brought on by poor lifestyle choices and heredity. If such diseases can be detected earlier, then proper lifestyle choices and treatment plans can save the lives of many people around the world. The goal of this study is to accurately detect patients by applying machine learning models like K-Nearest Neighbors, Support Vector Machine, Logistic Regression, Gaussian Naive Bayes, AdaBoost, and XGBoost. This research presents a hybrid machine learning model that promotes sensitivity over specificity. The suggested hybrid model, which combines bagged Logistic Regression with hyperparameter-optimized KNN, performs better than either algorithm alone, with 79% accuracy and 88% sensitivity. Additionally, this study will raise awareness among people in various age groups who are at higher risk for coronary heart disease, encouraging them to examine their heart health and take the necessary precautions to prevent premature death.

Keywords: Coronary Heart disease · K-Nearest Neighbors · Logistic Regression · Hybrid model · Early prediction

1 Introduction

Coronary heart disease (CHD) occurs when arteries in the heart become blocked due to the buildup of plaque, hindering the continuous supply of oxygen-rich blood. This restriction of blood flow can lead to heart attacks, making CHD a pernicious condition often referred to as a "silent" killer. It is important to note that blood clotting does not happen suddenly but develops over time. CHD manifests in two forms. The chronic form involves a gradual narrowing of the coronary arteries, leading to persistent symptoms such as chest pain, shortness of breath, nausea, and discomfort in the arms or shoulders. On the other hand, the sudden form poses an acute medical emergency, where plaque rupture results in the rapid formation of a blood clot that obstructs blood flow, causing a heart attack.

© The Author(s), under exclusive license to Springer Nature Switzerland AG 2024
D. Herath et al. (Eds.): APANConf 2023, CCIS 1995, pp. 63–75, 2024.
https://doi.org/10.1007/978-3-031-51135-6_6

Research conducted in the United States indicates that CHD accounts for approximately 1 in 7 deaths, with a heart attack occurring every 40 s [1]. In New Zealand, the prevalence of CHD is significant, with 1 in 20 individuals affected, and heart-related diseases claiming a life every 90 min [4]. This type of heart disease is the most prevalent. Although specific data on the number of CHD patients in Bangladesh is not available, a study examining CHD prevalence in the adult Bangladeshi population found the highest reported prevalence to be 21%, with urban areas exhibiting a weighted pooled prevalence of 8% compared to 2% in rural areas [2]. Moreover, a 2020 study by the World Health Organization(WHO) reported that CHD contributed to 108,528 deaths in Bangladesh, accounting for 15.16% of total deaths and ranking it second among the Top 50 Causes of Death [3]. While genetics can play a role in CHD, lifestyle factors are considered significant contributors to the development of non-communicable diseases.

This paper comprehensively analyzes various models and presents research findings that shed light on the performance of Hybrid Machine Learning Models in predicting CHD. Extensive review of existing research papers has greatly assisted this study. Hopefully, this paper will similarly contribute to future research by providing a valuable collection of findings on CHD and its early prediction.

1.1   Objective of the Study

The objective of this study is to address the complexity and precision required in medical diagnosis, particularly in the challenging task of predicting coronary heart disease (CHD). Existing surveys conducted by the WHO reveal that medical professionals achieve only 67% accuracy in predicting CHD.

To enhance the predictive capabilities in the medical field, the use of Machine Learning (ML) techniques offers valuable insights from vast datasets. While previous research has explored CHD detection using historical datasets, this study delves deeper by employing hybrid ML models, aiming to contribute to future advancements in the field. The specific objectives of this proposed system are as follows, designed to benefit CHD researchers:

- Conduct proper data pre-processing to ensure data quality and reliability.
- Train and test various ML algorithms individually, eliminating models with lower accuracy.
- Fine-tune the hyperparameters of the selected models to optimize their performance.
- Employ ensemble techniques to combine the individual models into hybrid models, enhancing overall accuracy and sensitivity.

By pursuing these objectives, this research aims to advance the understanding and prediction of CHD, offering valuable insights to researchers and practitioners in the field.

2   Related Work

Several research studies have been conducted on the prognosis and early detection of heart disease using ML algorithms. Yadav et al. conducted a study that achieved high accuracy rates using Neural Network (98%) and Fuzzy KNN (94.19%) algorithms, outperforming other algorithms [5]. Another study focused on early heart disease detection and achieved an accuracy of 87.5%, with KNN and Logistic Regression outperforming Random Forest Classifier [6]. By focusing on the sensitivity rate, Naïve Bayes outperforms Support Vector Machine, and Decision Tree algorithms by demonstrating the highest 63% [7].

A study has employed KNN and Random Forest algorithms, with KNN showing superior accuracy (86.885%) [8]. Another research has evaluated several algorithms and found that Random Forest achieved the highest scores in accuracy (83.51%), precision (88.89%), AUC (88.24%), and F1 score (84.21%) [9]. A hybrid model has been proposed in a research combining Decision Tree and Random Forest, achieving an accuracy of 88% [10]. By applying Random Forest algorithm, Motarwar et al. obtained a highest 95.08% accuracy rate [11].

A research has utilized Relief and LASSO feature selection techniques, finding Random Forest to perform well with accuracy ranging from 92.65% to 99.05% [12]. Another study focused on CHD detection and achieved high accuracy rates, with KNN, Decision Tree, and Random Forest reaching 100% accuracy [13]. Kumar et al. reported an accuracy of 85.71% using Random Forest, with an AUC score of 0.8765 [14].

These studies highlight the effectiveness of various machine learning algorithms in predicting and detecting heart disease.

3   Methodology

3.1   Dataset

We obtain our dataset from an online repository called KEEL [15]. The dataset, named 'South African Heart Dataset', originally contains 462 instances, containing 9 independent variables or features which are: Systolic blood pressure (Sbp), Cumulative tobacco in kg (tobacco), Bad Cholesterol also known as Low Density Lipoprotein (LDL), Adiposity, Family history of heart disease (famhist), Type-A behavior (typea), Obesity, Current alcohol consumption (alcohol), Age at onset (age). The dataset has one dependent (target) variable. The target class contains two outcomes: 0 and 1 where '0' indicates that the person does not have CHD and '1' indicates that the person has CHD.

3.2   Data Pre-processing

Firstly, the dataset was converted from its original '.dat' format to '.csv' format for improved manageability. String values within the dataset were then transformed into binary values using the "LabelEncoder" module from the scikit-learn library.

To train and test the models effectively, the dataset was split using the "train-test-split" module, with 85% allocated for training and 15% for testing, surpassing the conventional 80% train size. Addressing the issue of class imbalance, both oversampling and undersampling techniques were employed in separate experiments. For oversampling, the Synthetic Minority Over-sampling Technique (SMOTE) was utilized, generating 120 synthetic instances with CHD-Positive ('1') labels to balance the training dataset, making a total of 582 instances in the dataset whereas it had originally 462 instances. Conversely, the Edited Nearest Neighbors (ENN) algorithm was applied for undersampling, removing 149 observations labeled with CHD-Negative ('0') from the training dataset, making a total of 313 instances from the original 462 instances in the original dataset. Lastly, to mitigate the discrepancy in feature scales, particularly notable between "Sbp" with a mean value of 139.99 and "famhist" with 0.42, the'StandardScaler' module from the scikit-learn library was employed for data standardization, effectively eliminating the bias caused by scale differences. To better demonstrate the work flow, a diagram (Fig. 1) has been provided to demonstrate the process.

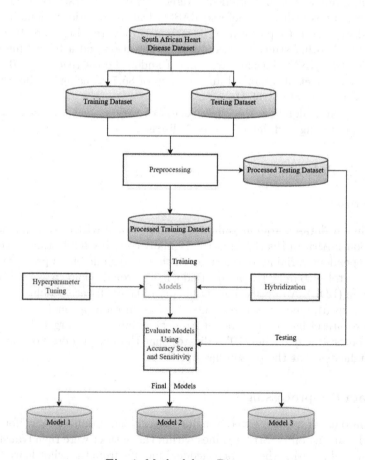

Fig. 1. Methodology Diagram.

3.3   Classifiers

The dataset has been trained with the following Machine Learning models:

- K-Nearest Neighbors
- Support Vector Machine
- Logistic Regression
- Gaussian Naïve Bayes
- AdaBoost
- XGBoost

4   Result

4.1   Performance Analysis

After conducting a literature review, the focus of this research has been based on a specific paper titled "Prediction of CHD using Machine Learning: An Experimental Analysis" [7]. The paper employed Naïve Bayes, Support Vector Machine (SVM), and Decision Tree algorithms. The goal of this research was to improve the accuracy and sensitivity by using the same dataset [15]. So the dataset used in our study is the same dataset used in an existing work [7]. The chosen algorithms were K-Nearest Neighbors, Support Vector Machine, Logistic Regression, Gaussian Naïve Bayes, AdaBoost, and XGBoost.

The initial accuracy and sensitivity of individual models, without using any sampling techniques, are shown below (Fig. 2):

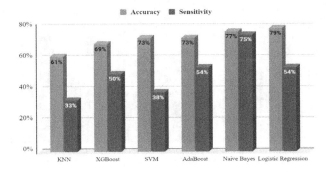

Fig. 2. Initial List of Models (Without using SMOTE).

Due to the imbalanced dataset, most of the models showed unsatisfactory results in sensitivity score. To address this issue, the SMOTE oversampling technique has been applied to balance the dataset. And the following results has been achieved (Fig. 3):

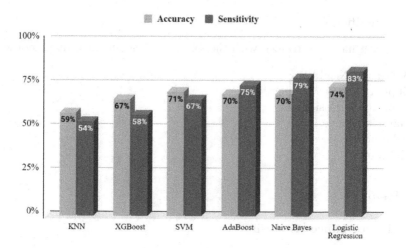

Fig. 3. Initial List of Models (Using SMOTE).

It is to be noted that, no sampling techniques were used the existing work on the dataset [7], making our approach novel and unique.

The subsequent phase of the analysis was hyperparameter optimization. The following results were yielded (Fig. 4):

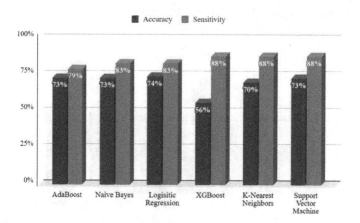

Fig. 4. Hyperparameter Tuned Models.

As a result of the hyperparameter optimization, some models did better in accuracy and sensitivity. To create hybrid models using well-performing individual models, the poor performing algorithms were eliminated. For each model, Randomized Search and Grid Search algorithms have been applied to find the best combination of hyperparameters. It should be emphasized that the Logistic

Regression model did not perform any better when using the best combinations found by the search algorithms than when default hyperparameters were used. The hyperparameters of each model are displayed below (Table 1):

Table 1. Performance Comparison Among Existing Research Works.

Model	Hyperparameters
AdaBoost	learning_rate = 0.1 n_estimators = 50
Naive Bayes	var_smoothing = 0.12328467394420659
XGBoost	n_estimators = 10 max_depth = 1 learning_rate = 0.01 subsample = 1.0 colsample_bytree = 0.7
KNN	leaf_size = 1 n_neighbors = 30 weights = 'distance' metric = 'minkowski'
SVC	C = 1.8504421136977791 gamma = 0.0011970424904099205 probability = True
Logistic Regression	penalty = 'none' solver = 'newton-cg'

In the following phase, to construct hybrid models, ensemble techniques has been employed, specifically the Bagging Classifier and Voting Classifier from the scikit-learn library. With the Bagging Classifier, the Bagging technique to each individual model has been applied, resembling the creation of a hybrid model like Random Forest, which combines multiple Decision Trees. Additionally, utilizing the Voting Classifier, two distinct models have been to form a hybrid model, ensuring superior performance compared to the individual models. Experiments with both soft voting and hard voting methods has been conducted to determine the optimal approach.

Upon implementing the Bagging technique, a superior performing hybrid model has been identified in comparison to the other models. Consequently, hyperparameter optimization has been performed specifically for this model, resulting in marginal improvement in accuracy. The performance of the models is presented below (Fig. 5):

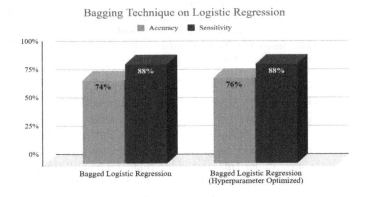

Fig. 5. Bagging Technique on Logistic Regression.

The hyperparameters of the hyperparameter-optimized bagged Logistic Regression are:

- Logistic Regression Base Model: C=1
- Bagging Classifier: max_features=0.7, max_samples=0.5, n_estimators=1000

While using Voting Classifier, a python dictionary has been used to store all the models including the default ones, optimized ones and the bagged ones, after which the dictionary has been looped through to find the best combination of models, along with the best voting type (either soft or hard). Through extensive experimentation with diverse model combinations, successful identification of the following top-performing models among the various configurations has been achieved (Table 2 and Fig. 6):

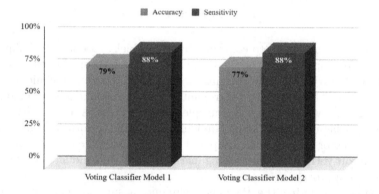

Fig. 6. Voting Classifier Models.

Below is a description of the models shown above:

Table 2. Voting Classifiers.

Models	Combination	Voting Type
Voting Classifier Model 1	Hyperparameter-optimized KNN and Bagged Logistic Regression	Hard
Voting Classifier Model 2	Default Logistic Regression and Hyperparameter-optimized Naive Bayes	Soft

After conducting the aforementioned experiments with an 85%–15% train-test split using the SMOTE oversampling method, another experiment has been conducted with a 70%–30% train-test split while maintaining the same configurations and models. The purpose of this experiment was to evaluate the performance of the models under this particular split. Among all the models in our list, the hyperparameter-optimized XGBoost model has been identified as the best performer using the aforementioned configuration (Fig. 7).

After conducting the aforementioned experiments using the SMOTE oversampling technique on the dataset, an additional experiment has been further

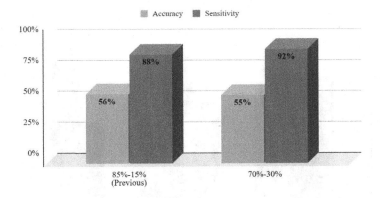

Fig. 7. XGBoost (Tuned) Model using Different Train-test Splits.

conducted with an 85%–15% train-test split, utilizing the ENN undersampling technique on the dataset as initially planned. All other configurations, including the models, remained unchanged. This experiment aimed to assess the performance of the models with different sampling techniques applied to the training dataset.

Among all the models evaluated, the following AdaBoost model (with default hyperparameters) has been identified as the best performer after employing the Edited Nearest Neighbors undersampling technique (Fig. 8):

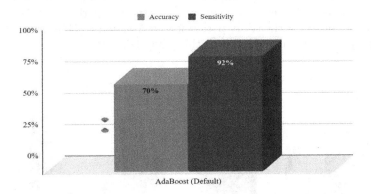

Fig. 8. AdaBoost Model using ENN.

Based on the outcomes of our extensive experimentation, three models has been identified that emerged as the top performers, with the sensitivity score serving as the primary performance metric. These models have been ranked from 1 to 3, the first in rank being the proposed model (Fig. 9).

While the sensitivity score has been emphasized as the primary evaluation metric throughout the research, it has also been included the specificity score in this ranked list to provide a more comprehensive picture of the performance of the models. Despite having the lowest sensitivity score among the three models,

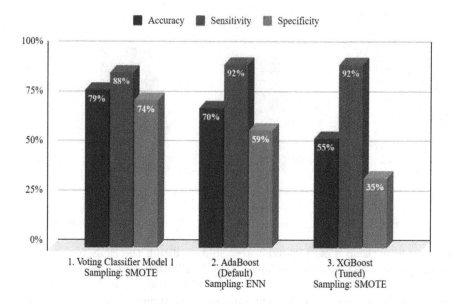

Fig. 9. Top Performing Models (Ranked).

the Voting Classifier Model 1 has been selected as the proposed model due to its ability to strike a fine balance between sensitivity and specificity.

In order to gain a more comprehensive understanding of the performance of these models, following is a comparison of the top performing models with the proposed model of the study performed by Amanda H. Gonsalves, et al. [7], where they used the same dataset as this study (Fig. 10):

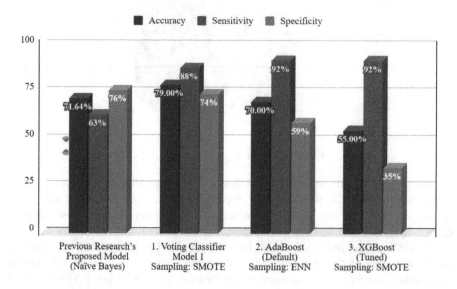

Fig. 10. Top Performing Models (Comparison Between Two Studies).

Upon analyzing the comparison of our proposed model (Voting Classifier Model 1) with the Naive Bayes model which was the proposed model of the study performed by Amanda H. Gonsalves, et al. [7], it becomes evident that this proposed model excels in both accuracy and sensitivity score. However, it is important to note that in terms of specificity score, the proposed model is marginally lower than the Naive Bayes model. Moreover, the primary focus throughout the research process was on achieving a higher sensitivity score rather than maximizing specificity. This decision was based on the nature of the research question and the goal of the analysis. Hence, the superior performance of this proposed model in accuracy and sensitivity score compensates for any marginal decrease in specificity score.

4.2   Result Evaluation

Following is the classification report of our top performing models (Fig. 11):

Performance Metrics	Target Labels	1. Voting Classifier Model 1	2. AdaBoost (Sampling: ENN)	3. XGBoost (Split: 70%-30%)
Precision	0	92%	93%	89%
	1	64%	54%	43%
	Macro Average	78%	73%	66%
	Weighted Average	82%	80%	73%
Recall	0	74%	59%	35%
	1	88%	92%	92%
	Macro Average	81%	75%	63%
	Weighted Average	79%	70%	55%
F1-Score	0	82%	72%	50%
	1	74%	68%	58%
	Macro Average	78%	70%	54%
	Weighted Average	79%	71%	53%
Accuracy		**79%**	**70%**	**55%**

Fig. 11. Classification Report.

Following are the confusion matrices of our top performing models (Fig. 12):

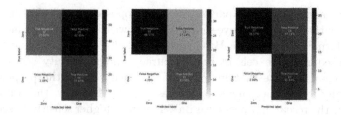

Fig. 12. Confusion Matrices of Voting Classifier Model 1, AdaBoost (Sampling: ENN) and XGBoost (Split: 70–30).

5   Conclusion and Future Work

The devastating toll of heart diseases necessitates the incorporation of machine learning techniques alongside traditional medical approaches to effectively combat this lethal ailment. By synchronising human expertise with machine intelligence, most of the world population can collectively overcome the challenges posed by CHD and other life-threatening diseases. And with this idea in mind, it has been seen in this research how Hybrid Machine Learning Models can contribute to this cause. By incorporating some Data Preprocessing techniques and other techniques, it has helped Hybrid Models learn and predict in an efficient manner. In the end, 3 better performing models have been found in comparison with every other models. And the best among them, according to selection process, was a Voting Classifier Model that had an accuracy score of 79%, sensitivity score of 88%, and specificity score of 74%. There are many creative possibilities in this field in using hybrid machine learning models.

Looking ahead, future research endeavors could prioritize the refinement of hybrid models to strike a delicate balance between sensitivity and specificity, ensuring comprehensive diagnostic capabilities. Additionally, the limited availability of heart disease datasets on a global scale necessitates the exploration of Synthetic Data generation Techniques, as demonstrated in a breast cancer study conducted by M. S. K. Inan, et al., [16]. Leveraging such techniques would enable enhanced learning and prediction capabilities, thereby revolutionizing CHD management and prevention strategies. Furthermore, efforts can be made for developing a smartphone application dedicated to CHD prediction and assessment, with the additional feature that evaluates and informs which patient attributes are at abnormal levels, causing the positive CHD prediction. By persistently advancing and innovating in these domains, remarkable advancements can be achieved in the realm of CHD healthcare, significantly improving patient outcomes and well-being.

References

1. Heart disease facts. https://theheartfoundation.org/heart-disease-facts-2/. Accessed 24 Dec 2022
2. Chowdhury, M., et al.: Prevalence of cardiovascular disease among Bangladeshi adult population: a systematic review and meta-analysis of the studies. Vascular Health Risk Manage. **14**, 165–181 (2018)
3. Coronary heart disease in Bangladesh. https://www.worldlifeexpectancy.com/ bangladesh-coronary-heart-disease. Accessed 26 Dec 2022
4. Coronary heart disease - symptoms, causes and treatment. https://www. southerncross.co.nz/medical-library/heart-conditions/coronary-heart-disease-symptoms-causes-and-treatment. Accessed 24 Dec 2022
5. Yadav, S.S., Jadhav, S.M., Nagrale, S., Patil, N.: Application of machine learning for the detection of heart disease. In: 2020 2nd International Conference on Innovative Mechanisms for Industry Applications (ICIMIA) (2020)
6. Jindal, H., Agrawal, S., Khera, R., Jain, R., Nagrath, P.: Heart disease prediction using machine learning algorithms. IOP Conf. Ser. Mater. Sci. Eng. **1022**, 012072 (2021)
7. Gonsalves, A.H., Thabtah, F., Mohammad, R.M., Singh, G.: Prediction of coronary heart disease using machine learning. In: Proceedings of the 2019 3rd International Conference on Deep Learning Technologies (2019)
8. Garg, A., Sharma, B., Khan, R.: Heart disease prediction using Machine Learning Techniques. IOP Conf. Ser. Mater. Sci. Eng. **1022**, 012046 (2021)
9. Sujatha, P., Mahalakshmi, K.: Performance evaluation of supervised machine learning algorithms in prediction of heart disease. In: 2020 IEEE International Conference for Innovation in Technology (INOCON) (2020)
10. Kavitha, M., Gnaneswar, G., Dinesh, R., Sai, Y.R., Suraj, R.S.: Heart disease prediction using Hybrid Machine Learning Model. In: 2021 6th International Conference on Inventive Computation Technologies (ICICT) (2021)
11. Motarwar, P., Duraphe, A., Suganya, G., Premalatha, M.: Cognitive approach for heart disease prediction using machine learning. In: 2020 International Conference on Emerging Trends in Information Technology and Engineering (ic-ETITE) (2020)
12. Ghosh, P., et al.: Efficient prediction of cardiovascular disease using machine learning algorithms with relief and lasso feature selection techniques. IEEE Access. **9**, 19304–19326 (2021)
13. Ali, M.M., Paul, B.K., Ahmed, K., Bui, F.M., Quinn, J.M.W., Moni, M.A.: Heart disease prediction using supervised machine learning algorithms: performance analysis and comparison. Comput. Biol. Med. **136**, 104672 (2021)
14. Kumar, N.K., Sindhu, G.S., Prashanthi, D.K., Sulthana, A.S.: Analysis and prediction of cardio vascular disease using machine learning classifiers. In: 2020 6th International Conference on Advanced Computing and Communication Systems (ICACCS) (2020)
15. South African Heart data set. https://sci2s.ugr.es/keel/dataset.php?cod=184. Accessed 24 Dec 2022
16. Inan, M.S., Hossain, S., Uddin, M.N.: Data augmentation guided breast cancer diagnosis and prognosis using an integrated deep-generative framework based on breast tumor's morphological information. Inf. Med. Unlocked **37**, 101171 (2023)

Design and Development of Real-Time IIoT for Multi-cloud Factory Vehicle Monitoring System

Patchapong Kulthumrongkul[1]($\boxtimes$), Papat Fungthanmasarn[2], and Chaodit Asawakul[1]

[1] Wireless Network and Future Internet Research Unit, Department of Electrical Engineering, Faculty of Engineering, Chulalongkorn University, Bangkok, Thailand
`6230361921@student.chula.ac.th`
[2] Jenbunjerd Innovation Center, Jenbunjerd Co., Ltd., Nonthaburi, Thailand

Abstract. Material handling equipment, such as forklifts, is broadly used in many industries to increase the efficiency of production. However, if the equipment unexpectedly breaks down, then that can potentially interrupt the overall manufacturing. Therefore, it is beneficial to the industry if the equipment usage data can be monitored in real time so that responsible engineers can identify faults before they occur. In this research, a prototype for a factory vehicle monitoring system has been designed and implemented. The proposed solution is to acquire real-time usage data from the motor drive of the factory vehicle and send the data to the cloud via narrowband IoT which is a low-power wide area network. The received real-time data streams can be visualized on the monitoring website to observe the status of the vehicles. The solution is attained with multiple clouds appropriately chosen according to their offering services, which include telecommunication cloud, public cloud and on-premise cloud. The experiment has been performed to verify that the monitored data can explain actual data during the actual operation within an actual factory environment. Additionally, the example of a monitoring website is given to present the utility of the website to monitor the status of the vehicles.

Keywords: Industrial Internet of Things · Real-Time Monitoring System · Cloud

1 Introduction

To improve intralogistics performance, material handling equipment (MHE) is widely employed in many different sectors. MHE (e.g. in factory vehicles and forklifts) facilitates reducing operational times and increasing production, particularly in the warehouse. MHE leasing companies or factories usually want to prolong the MHE lifespan by proper controls for the use of vehicles [6]. Vehicle faults could result from consumer abuse or vehicle-leasing contract violations. The failure interrupts overall production and results in unexpected downtime.

© The Author(s), under exclusive license to Springer Nature Switzerland AG 2024
D. Herath et al. (Eds.): APANConf 2023, CCIS 1995, pp. 76–85, 2024.
https://doi.org/10.1007/978-3-031-51135-6_7

Such vehicle failure consequences can be mitigated at the early stages of a vehicle malfunction and that should be identifible by collecting real-time usage data using industrial internet of things (IIoT) technology [11].

The IIoT plays an important role in the monitoring system. This technology deployment often begins with perception layers, which sense environmental characteristics of operating MHE and then transmit preprocessed data to the application part via a communication protocol to represent that information in meaningful ways [13]. In order to retrieve vehicle parameters, a data acquisition system should be implemented on the MHE motor drive. The network connection is one of the challenges of implementing IIoT since its capacity will influence the performance of IIoT devices [5]. This is because the MHE can be leased to or used at several operating sites where a network connection is still necessary. In addition, the MHE usually travels across numerous zones in the warehouse. Therefore, the narrow-band Internet of Things (NB-IoT), one of the low power wide area networks (LPWANs), is taken into consideration. At a reasonable cost in the present market, NB-IoT supports large coverage areas for both outdoor and even indoor environments, requires low energy consumption and enables massive device connections at once [5, 9, 17].

Applications for the IIoT normally combine cloud computing as an essential component for enhancing the effectiveness of monitoring services such as data processing, storage, or service deployment [20]. As a result, one can develop software, such as monitoring websites or alerting systems, to usefully display information from sensor nodes. The services can be launched in the cloud with container technology which isolates the applications and programming dependencies from the infrastructure, and hence, lightweight and portable functionalities between clouds [19]. In addition, if a massive amount of IIoT data is gathered, cloud computing can also help facilitate an increase in computation workload by a properly engineered pay-as-you-go model. With cloud enablements, one can deal with any required computation and thus facilitate on necessary real-time or non-real-time control decisions [18].

There are several pieces of research that aim to monitor the status of electric vehicles (EVs) by applying IIoT technologies. In [10], the battery condition of the EV has been monitored by setting up the external sensors and sending the data to the cloud via Wi-Fi. A prototype of a remote condition monitoring system of CAN vehicles has been implemented such that the user can access the live data through the mobile application [14]. The design of a battery management system based on IoT and CAN BUS has been proposed to monitor the operating conditions of the battery [16]. These papers concentrate on the battery state monitoring of typical EVs with CAN protocol while the in-factory vehicles with different communication protocols including Universal Asynchronous Receiver-Transmitter (UART) protocol are barely focused. Therefore, this study focuses on the design and development of a full-stack system prototype to monitor the status of the in-factory vehicles by applying IIoT and cloud technologies. Key design factors have been reported in this paper, based on the actual implementation of a prototype system that has been tested in a real factory environment, as follows:

– How to accurately and reliably obtain the usage data from the motor drive of an in-factory vehicle and how to check its functionality comparatively to sensors internally installed inside the motor drive which can be diagnosed with a standard offline handheld device.
– How to communicate between devices and the clouds including the telecommunication cloud, public cloud and on-premise cloud
– How to design the full-stack application to visualize the significant information or how the value of the data should be elevated

2   Design of Real-Time IIoT for Multi-cloud Factory Vehicle Monitoring System

2.1   System Architecture

The architecture of the factory vehicle monitoring system (see Fig. 1) consists of 5 main components including the physical part, telecommunication (Telco) cloud, on-premise cloud, public cloud and application. The IIoT devices and different cloud servers provide a good quality of service and increase the reliability of the system. Different cloud service providers are chosen according to their corresponding services offered. In Telco cloud, Magellan [2], an IoT cloud platform, has the sensor/controller gateway responsibility to receive data from the microcontroller and forward to other services. On-premise cloud deals with the deployment of the front-end and the back-end server for enhanced time-responsiveness of user interfaces and lastly, the public cloud has been selected for its available secured and most reliable database service. With multiple clouds integrated, it may increase the complexity of service integration. However, in the wide-area deployment of IIoT, such complexity can be worthy to exploit distinct advantages of different service features offered by those clouds.

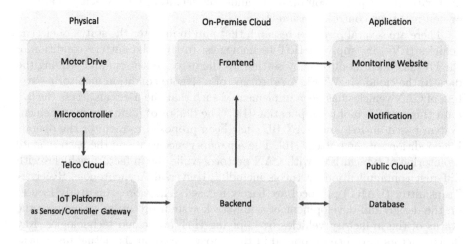

Fig. 1. Factory vehicle monitoring system architecture.

2.2   Selection of Hardware and Software Components

In the prototype being developed in this research Curtis 1212S [4] motor speed controller has been chosen with 18 parameters that can be monitored during MHE operation (see Fig. 2). The DEVIO NB-DEVKIT I (Devio) [1] has been selected as a microcontroller integrated with the NB-IoT connection on board. Moreover, this board has an esp32-based processor which can be developed through the Arduino IDE platform or Platform IO. In order to communicate between Devio and the motor drive, the converter is needed to switch the signal between RS232 and Transistor-Transistor Logic (TTL) protocol. Devio requires an input voltage of 5V DC that can be stepped down from the 24V battery of MHE. The installation of IIoT device is shown in Fig. 3.

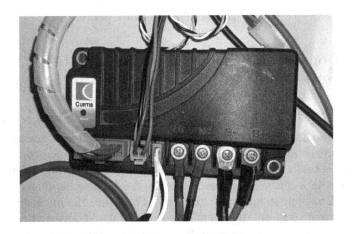

Fig. 2. Curtis1212S motor drive controller.

In software platform selection, Magellan [2] is herein used to support Devio because of its service availability provided by the selected Telco service provider. Additionally, the Magellan platform provides libraries that can automatically connect to the network and Magellan. Hence, it is convenient to implement the system of sensor/controller gateway functionality. Next, AWS DynamoDB [3] is chosen to be the database because of its security and reliability in the public cloud and readiness of software development kit (SDK) for developers. The on-premise cloud is based at this prototyping stage in the IoTcloudServe@TEIN containerized cloud [8]. The back-end manages the application programming interfaces (API) using Flask [7], a Python web framework and the front-end has been at full-stack developed in this research by using ReactJS [15] - an open-source JavaScript library for building web applications. Lastly, the notification system is applied on Line Notify [12].

Fig. 3. The installation of IIoT device.

3   Functional Components of Real-Time IIoT for Multi-cloud Factory Vehicle Monitoring System

3.1   Data Acquisition System

In order to monitor the status of vehicles, the usage data streams of sensor readings from the motor drive have to be collected by the microcontroller. The motor drive actually has the usage data, such as battery voltage or motor voltage, and this data can be monitored by a standard offline handheld device, but without API to request for sensor readings. Therefore, the microcontroller has been programmed customarily to emulate such handheld device's ports by sending request packets and interpreting the responses. These packets represent the array of bytes sent between the diagnostic port of the motor drive and the software serial of the microcontroller. After receiving all parameters from the motor drive and the other sensors, including the GPS sensor and ambient sensors, it will send the payload to Magellan. These tasks will perform concurrently to satisfy the requirements (see Algorithm 1). The accuracy of the microcontroller-based emulator program has been confirmed by comparing directly to the sensor reading data with those readable from the standard offline handheld device. The reliability of this hardware interfacing part has been realised by the proper design of a watchdog sub-routine, which keeps checking norm operations and resets hardware when unexpected events occur. Based on the test results, the system being developed here can run reliably in checking accurate motor drive sensor readings.

3.2   Database System

To secure data in a database, Magellan has to forward the received data to DynamoDB running inside a public commercial cloud (here at AWS [3]). In Magellan, we can automatically send the data by implementing push mode which is

---

Algorithm 1: Gather real-time usage data and send it to Magellan

---

```
 1  do in parallel
 2  |   while true do
 3  |   |   for all parameters do
 4  |   |   |   Send Request Packet
 5  |   |   |   Delay - avoid noise (20ms)
 6  |   |   |   Receive Response Packet
 7  |   |   |   Decode the packet to retrieve parameter
 8  |   |   |   Delay between parameter (20ms)
 9  |   |   end for
10  |   |   Check the validity of the data
11  |   |   Delay - call this task every 5s
12  |   end while
13  |   while true do
14  |   |   Get timestamp
15  |   |   Assign flag
16  |   |   Generate Payload
17  |   |   Send to Magellan
18  |   |   if Data is available then
19  |   |   |   Delay - call this task every 10s
20  |   |   else
21  |   |   |   Delay - call this task every minute
22  |   |   end if
23  |   end while
24  |   while true do
25  |   |   Read on board Sensor
26  |   |   Read onboard humidity
27  |   |   Read GPS location
28  |   |   Delay - call this task every 5s
29  |   end while
30  end
```

---

event-based forwarding. Magellan will forward the data to a user endpoint whenever the data is received. This push, not pulling, mode of operational design helps increase the reliability of the system with fewer missing data points readable thanks to this data streamlining method.

After the back-end obtains data from Magellan, it will select the data and format it to be the same as in the target schema predefined in the database. Because DynamoDB is a key-value database, the partition key and sort key have to be matched with formatted data. Then, it will put the formatted data into the database.

3.3   Back-End and Front-End Servers

The back-end server is dealing with all computations in the cloud. The most significant part of the back-end server is how to design APIs to raise the efficiency of the monitoring system. To improve the capability, the back-end server can also locally cache the repeated data and update it when required. This will reduce the amount of data transmission and the number of read requests and consequently decrease the service cost of the public cloud. After the data is processed, the front-end visualizes the data with the designed user interfaces on the monitoring website. The lists of APIs are split into three sections according to the data responsible for each section.

The first section is authentication. Every user has a role that identifies the service in the monitoring website that the user can reach. Therefore, the user's role will be stored in the session. The session remains active until the user logs out. The second section is motor drive data. This is the most important part of the monitoring system. The user, whose role can monitor the usage data, is accessible to view records of the vehicle operation, for example, the latest data of each vehicle, or the historical data of that vehicle. The last section is device management. Since the IIoT equipment is installed on the vehicle, the mapping between the IIoT devices and the vehicle is necessary by matching the serial number of hardware devices installed within individual in-factory vehicles.

4   Experimental Results of Prototype Functionality Test

To verify the reliability of the acquisition system, data from the handheld and data from the monitoring system have been compared. The experiment has been set up with the actual MHE with two motor drives to control the left and right wheels of the test vehicle. The developed microcontroller hardware set has been installed at one of the motor drives, while the offline handheld monitoring device is at the other. To compare readings from the two methods, the vehicle has been moved in a straight line. Therefore, those motor drives will have a similar electrical loading scenario during the operation. While moving forward, motor voltage and armature current have been recorded and herein depicted as a comparison between the ground truth data as manually collected by a handheld device, and the monitored data as obtained from the developed cloud-based system (see Fig. 4).

The outcomes show that the monitored data can consistently capture the dynamics of the actual data with a measurable delay time in the order of up to 10 s. This is because the motor drive sensor reading task running on the microcontroller is called periodically through the developed hardware interface every 10 s. Despite of such latency, this system has no need to get exact real-time data synchronization to make remotely actuating control decisions. Thus, the latency of obtaining monitored data in this order is practically acceptable. The related ranges of the data can show that the system has capability sufficiently considered as real-time monitoring the status of MHEs. The collected data are also shown on the monitoring website, which is a convenient way to track the condition of the vehicles. An example of a device dashboard that provides important vehicle information is displayed (see Fig. 5). The developed system can thus empower the in-factory vehicle leasing company or the factory's operational control room to sustain their critical manufacturing or warehouse operations.

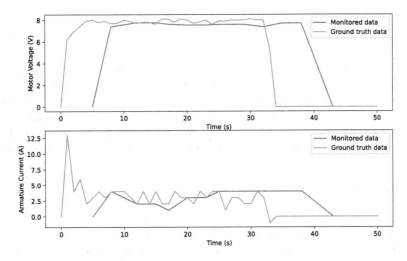

Fig. 4. Comparison between ground truth data manually collected by a handheld device and monitored data as obtained from developed cloud-based system.

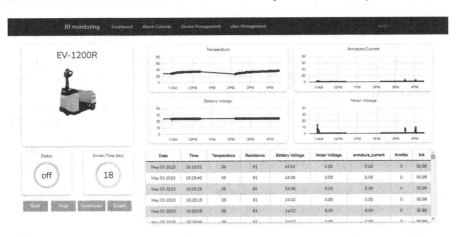

Fig. 5. An example of device dashboard.

5 Conclusion

In this paper, the real-time in-factory vehicle monitoring system has been successfully developed in order to track the status of MHE during operation. The designed microcontroller has the ability to repeatedly obtain real-time usage data from the motor drive of the in-factory vehicle and send the data to the cloud. With the integration of multiple cloud services, the data are feasible to display on the monitoring website. The verification of the monitored data from the prototype functionality test shows that the monitored data is sufficiently reliable for capturing the actual operating data with the delay time of up to 10 s. As a result, the industry as well as vehicle leasing companies can take advantage of the system to improve operational performance by detecting and identifying the unusual patterns of monitored data that may lead to the unexpected breakdown of the operating vehicle. To prevent vehicle failure, in future work, condition monitoring or predictive maintenance could be implemented on the back-end server running on the cloud and incorporated with the alerting system to notify the user of vehicle upkeep. The statistical learning methods are therefore essential for the decision-making to decide the optimal period for maintenance. Thus, the industry will achieve better quality of service from the monitoring system.

References

1. AIS IoT Alliance Program: DEVIO NB-DEVKIT I. https://aiap.ais.co.th/iotdevcenter/IoTDevice/DevioNBDevkit. Accessed 06 May 2023
2. AIS IoT Alliance Program: Magellan. https://magellan.ais.co.th/. Accessed 06 May 2023
3. Amazon Web Services: Amazon DynamoDB. https://aws.amazon.com/dynamodb. Accessed 06 May 2023
4. Curtis Instruments Inc: Manual model 1212s electronic motor controller. https://cdn.curtisinstruments.com/products/manuals/1212S_manual_en.pdf. Accessed 06 May 2023
5. Dangana, M., Ansari, S., Abbasi, Q.H., Hussain, S., Imran, M.A.: Suitability of nb-iot for indoor industrial environment: a survey and insights. Sensors **21**(16), 5284 (2021)
6. Falkenberg, S.F., Spinler, S.: The role of novel data in maintenance planning: breakdown predictions for material handling equipment. Comput. Ind. Eng. **169**, 108230 (2022)
7. Flask: Flask. https://flask.palletsprojects.com/en/2.3.x/. Accessed 06 May 2023
8. IoTcloudServe@TEIN: IoTcloudServe@TEIN. https://github.com/IoTcloudServe. Accessed 06 May 2023
9. Lauridsen, M., Kovács, I.Z., Mogensen, P., Sorensen, M., Holst, S.: Coverage and capacity analysis of lte-m and nb-iot in a rural area. In: 2016 IEEE 84th Vehicular Technology Conference (VTC-Fall), pp. 1–5. IEEE (2016)
10. Leksmi, S.S., Kumar, K.K., Vaz, F.A.J., Yuvarani, M.: Exploring innovative IoT solutions for automated battery condition detection in electric vehicles. In: 2023 7th International Conference on Computing Methodologies and Communication (ICCMC), pp. 1370–1375. IEEE (2023)
11. Li, Z., Fei, F., Zhang, G.: Edge-to-cloud IIoT for condition monitoring in manufacturing systems with ubiquitous smart sensors. Sensors **22**(15), 5901 (2022)
12. LINE Corporation©: LINE Notify. https://notify-bot.line.me/en/. Accessed 06 May 2023
13. Malik, P.K., et al.: Industrial internet of things and its applications in industry 4.0: state of the art. Comput. Commun. **166**, 125–139 (2021)
14. Medvedev, V., Butarovich, D., Smirnov, A.: Prototyping of the remote monitoring system of battery condition of the electric vehicle. J. Phys. Conf. Ser. **1177**, 012035 (2019)
15. Meta Open Source©: React. https://react.dev/. Accessed 06 May 2023

16. Pham, N.N., Leuchter, J., Pham, K.L., Dong, Q.H.: Battery management system for unmanned electric vehicles with can bus and internet of things. Vehicles **4**(3), 639–662 (2022)
17. Rastogi, E., Saxena, N., Roy, A., Shin, D.R.: Narrowband internet of things: a comprehensive study. Comput. Netw. **173**, 107209 (2020)
18. Wang, W., Hu, T., Gu, J.: Edge-cloud cooperation driven self-adaptive exception control method for the smart factory. Adv. Eng. Inform. **51**, 101493 (2022)
19. Yang, H., Ong, S., Nee, A., Jiang, G., Mei, X.: Microservices-based cloud-edge collaborative condition monitoring platform for smart manufacturing systems. Int. J. Prod. Res. **60**(24), 7492–7501 (2022)
20. Yu, W., Liu, Y., Dillon, T., Rahayu, W.: Edge computing-assisted IoT framework with an autoencoder for fault detection in manufacturing predictive maintenance. IEEE Trans. Industr. Inf. **19**(4), 5701–5710 (2022)

Towards True Decentralization: Development, Testing and Evaluation of a Novel Blockchain Consensus Protocol

Kesara Wimal[1]([✉]) [iD] and Geethapriya Liyanage[2] [iD]

[1] School of Computer Science and Engineering, University of Westminster, London, UK
w1851993@my.westminster.ac.uk
[2] Department of Computer Science and Engineering, University of
Moratuwa, Moratuwa, Sri Lanka

Abstract. The blockchain technology that powers the Bitcoin network was unveiled to the world in 2008. After more than a decade of research and development, a number of blockchain systems have been put out by both industry and academics. This research undertaking brings attention to a significant issue that impacts both blockchain users and cryptocurrency investors. The concern regarding true decentralization in existing blockchain platforms has long been a prominent topic within the blockchain community. Although Proof of Work (PoW), Proof of Stake (PoS), and hybrid approaches are commonly employed in blockchain systems, both methods exhibit limitations concerning decentralization. Despite the emergence of alternative consensus protocols, none have thus far achieved complete decentralization. This project aims to devise and implement an innovative consensus protocol that circumvents tendencies toward centralization, accommodates any number of network participants, eliminates the requirement for specialized hardware, reduces energy consumption, and fosters network activities. The proposed protocol advocates for a democratic and equitable approach to blockchain consensus. A comprehensive evaluation is conducted to assess the degree of achieved decentralization. The solution successfully demonstrates genuine decentralization. The test results also indicate enhanced security, and high performance, while obviating the need for specialized hardware and reducing energy consumption.

Keywords: Blockchain · Consensus Protocol · Distributed Ledger Technology · Decentralized Network · Security

1 Introduction

Satoshi Nakamoto's [1] whitepaper on Bitcoin introduced the concept of distributed blockchain in 2008. The paper provided an overview of the core ideas underlying a decentralized cryptocurrency system, laying the groundwork for later blockchain implementations. It outlined how a process known as mining, in which network users compete to solve challenging mathematical problems, verifies transactions and adds them

D. Herath et al. (Eds.): APANConf 2023, CCIS 1995, pp. 86–99, 2024.
https://doi.org/10.1007/978-3-031-51135-6_8

to the blockchain [2]. Due to its potential to transform numerous industries by enabling secure and transparent transactions, blockchain technology has attracted a lot of attention recently. Blockchain offers special capabilities that can be used in a variety of applications, from finance to healthcare and supply chain management [3].

The ability to reach a consensus among the participants is essential in the world of distributed systems, where several computers or nodes collaborate to complete a task [4]. Even in the event of failures or malevolent actors, consensus methods are crucial in guaranteeing that all nodes concur on a shared state or decision. Consensus procedures are crucial in the world of blockchain technology for maintaining the reliability and security of the decentralized network. Consensus protocols are tools that let users of a blockchain network come to an understanding of a single version of reality even in the absence of a central authority [5].

According to Shrivas et al. [6], existing consensus protocols enjoy widespread popularity and have undergone extensive testing. Nevertheless, they do not achieve complete decentralization as they are governed by a centralized authority. Additionally, certain protocols even discourage activities within the network, as noted by Ren [7]. Proof of Work (PoW), which is among the most popular protocols, demands specialized hardware resources and consumes a significant amount of energy, as highlighted by [8]. On the other hand, the second most popular protocol, Proof of Stake (PoS), necessitates a substantial stake to be held in order to be selected as a validator. This requirement acts as an entry barrier for many users, as pointed out by Ferdous et al. [9].

Over the period of time, members of the blockchain community have raised questions regarding the true decentralization of current blockchain platforms. Many popular blockchains employ either Proof of Work (PoW), Proof of Stake (PoS), or a combination of both. However, both PoW and PoS systems exhibit limitations in attaining complete decentralization [10]. A multitude of consensus protocols have emerged, each offering unique features and capabilities [11]. Nevertheless, none of these protocols have thus far achieved full decentralization and open participation, welcoming users of any level to become the next miner or forger in the system.

1.1 Research Contribution

The escalating prominence of blockchain technology has positioned it as a potentially transformative technology [12]. However, achieving complete decentralization in blockchain systems has proven to be a formidable challenge, given that many widely adopted consensus protocols initially designed to foster decentralization have eventually succumbed to the concentration of power. The case of Bitcoin serves as a prominent example, wherein discernible trends indicate a departure from its original, fully decentralized protocol toward increasing centralization. Consequently, it is crucial to approach any instances of centralization with circumspection, particularly in light of the susceptibility to a 51% attack [13]. This research assumes significance as it endeavors to contribute to the ongoing quest in the market for a genuinely decentralized protocol that effectively circumvents the consolidation of power.

This research project proposes a consensus mechanism that strives for true decentralization, ensuring that every user is granted an equal opportunity to mine the next block, irrespective of their wealth or available resources. Unlike PoS systems, this approach actively encourages network activities. Moreover, it eliminates the need for specialized hardware resources and does not consume a high amount of energy, as seen in PoW systems.

2 Background and Related Work

Blockchain technology has emerged as a disruptive innovation with the potential to revolutionize multiple sectors by providing safe and transparent data management solutions [14]. Functioning as a distributed ledger system, blockchain ensures secure and decentralized storage and verification of digital transactions, which are maintained by a network of computers rather than a single entity. Its core principles include decentralization, transparency, immutability, and consensus [15]. The concept of smart contracts, allowing for self-executing contracts with predefined rules inscribed into the blockchain, expanded the technology's applications following the publication of Nick Szabo's in 1996 [16]. This breakthrough has enabled trustless interactions and eliminated the need for intermediaries in various sectors like supply chain management, real estate, and decentralized banking.

The foundational premise of decentralized systems relies on consensus mechanisms to safeguard blockchain networks, given their pivotal role in ensuring security and integrity. Nonetheless, as decentralized technologies continue to gain widespread adoption, certain concerns have arisen related to current consensus protocols [17]. The existing body of literature encompasses a diverse range of studies and algorithms that have been developed to address the challenges associated with current consensus mechanisms [11]. Extensive research on decentralization in blockchains has primarily focused on Bitcoin [18]. These studies have pointed out that the emergence of mining pools has led to a tendency toward centralization in Bitcoin. While Bitcoin may exhibit a relatively higher degree of decentralization among its top miners, it is less decentralized overall [19].

The section presents a tabular exposition featuring a concise overview of the related work, delineating the synopsis, contributions, and limitations of each study (Table 1).

3 Design and Implementation

This section predominantly concentrates on delineating the design and implementation facets of the proposed system. Key design objectives encompass security, performance, usability, compatibility, and availability. These paramount goals are aimed at achieving a well-rounded system design. After careful consideration, the Structured Systems Analysis and Design Method (SSADM) was selected as the primary approach for constructing the solution, given that the anticipated language to be employed during implementation does not inherently support Object-Oriented Programming (OOP). This judicious decision was made to harmonize the development methodology with the language's constraints, thereby ensuring the development of an efficient and effective solution for the proposed system.

Table 1. Summary of existing work

Summary	Contributions	Limitations
The first survey paper explores alternative protocols for consensus algorithms, emphasizing their unique characteristics and degree of decentralization [20]	The study critically evaluates various alternative consensus algorithms, assessing their characteristics, advantages, and disadvantages	This study primarily examines consensus protocols proposed within only three years, with a stronger emphasis on academic papers over white papers
A decentralized consensus mechanism without proof of work, utilizing random selection to assign diverse validators for block proposals [21]	An innovative consensus protocol achieves true decentralization using game theory and randomness, addressing validator selection challenges by incentivizing truthful behavior	The protocol's initial design is intended for supply chain management and reveals the identities of leaders if they resubmit block proposals
A study highlights the importance of considering trustless platforms in the broader ecosystem with social and communication networks [22]	Minor network structure or dynamics changes can significantly disrupt the entire ecosystem's functioning. In interconnected socio-technical systems, these occurrences are expected to become more frequent	Findings are confined to a narrow range of scenarios and parameters, limiting the overall generalizability of the results
The research centered on validator committees with weighted block creation, and introduced updated voting profiles based on behavior, and aggregate blockchain rewards, using a multiplicative weights algorithm [23]	The introduced weighted voting enhances PoS consensus while enabling cost-effective testing, implementation, and reversion for existing users	The suggested solution may be limited to systems with few stacking nodes, and permissionless blockchain implementation could face challenges with the computational difficulty of building a profiling system
A study presented Delegated Proof of Reputation, a scalable, secure, and acceptably decentralized consensus protocol [24]	The innovative solution avoids redundant computation on old blocks from previous rating rounds and the partial reward incentivizes high decentralization in voting rounds	While some ranking theories may not be effective for blockchain ranking problems, DPoR remains resistant to loop attacks, yet requires additional measures to prevent boosting intentions

3.1 Algorithmic Design

The research project introduced a new consensus mechanism that is considered a valuable contribution as it provides a practical solution to a problem in the blockchain sector. The study extensively explores the question of whether blockchains are genuinely decentralized or if decentralization is merely a marketing tactic. In 2008, Nakamoto [1] provided an answer to the significant question of who would mine the next block through the introduction of the proof of work (PoW) consensus mechanism. The researchers propose a distinct approach to answering the same question, deviating from the reward-based mechanisms of PoW and PoS. Instead, their approach is based on punishment. By utilizing a punishment-based approach, the researchers argue that it can potentially enhance security, as the focus is not solely on rewards. However, it is worth noting that the study does not extensively discuss security aspects in detail.

A comprehensive discussion regarding the proposed consensus mechanism is elaborated upon in the subsequent section.

Genesis Block. The inaugural block, also known as the genesis block, is created by the first node that initiates the blockchain network. This block represents the sole instance in which no previous block hash exists within it. Upon its inception, the initial node is bestowed with 50 coins as an initial coin distribution. Nevertheless, it is worth noting that the protocol lacks a suitable mechanism for coin distribution, a limitation that will be further expounded upon in the concluding chapter of this research.

Complexity. The complexity of each individual block is denoted within its corresponding block header by a value that is always a power of 2. This complexity metric is determined by two distinct attributes.

1. Complexity of the previous block
2. Time consumed to produce the previous block

In the event that the preceding block required a duration greater than the block time this indicates that the complexity of that block was set too high. Consequently, the complexity of the subsequent block will be reduced by half of the previous complexity. Conversely, if the production time of the previous block was shorter than the block time this implies that the complexity level was too low. As a result, the complexity of the subsequent block will be augmented by twice the previous complexity.

Leader Election. The novel approach to finding the next forger or leader is straightforward. Every node in the network has its own mempool filled with new transactions and out of those each node will pick one transaction and vote for the creator of that transaction. The one who wins the election will be elected as the leader to forge the next block. Upon receipt of a number of transactions equivalent to the block's complexity, the voting process will commence.

Block Production. The block production process is initiated once a node receives votes equivalent to half the block complexity, at which point it assumes the role of leader for the ongoing block production process. Subsequently, the leader node will forge a block and disseminate it among its peers. The leader will drop transactions from nodes that have not broadcast their votes. This mechanism forces nodes to stay alive until their transaction is added to a block. Each node will accept the first block it receives and after the validation, the block will be added to its blockchain.

Block Time. The consensus protocol incorporates an inherent mechanism designed to ensure that the block time remains within a designated time frame. As previously explained, this time frame is dependent on the complexity attribute. The consensus mechanism proactively takes measures to constrain the block production time to a range of 30 to 90 s, with an average of approximately 1 min.

Penalty. Upon a node's detection of an invalid block being disseminated, it will proceed to broadcast information concerning the block's invalidity. If 51% of users are broadcasting about the invalid block the block producer will be penalized with his transaction value. The transactions will be added to a different mempool and will not be available to spend again in the future. There won't be any incentive for block production but nodes are forced to do it otherwise they won't be able to spend their transaction. This will reduce the malicious intent to gain the privileges of being the block creator. For a malicious node to successfully execute a double spending attack and reap the associated benefits, it must have control over 51% of the transaction senders. However, as the network expands, achieving such a degree of control becomes increasingly infeasible.

Flow Chart. The following flowchart illustrates the sequential flow of the algorithm (Fig. 1).

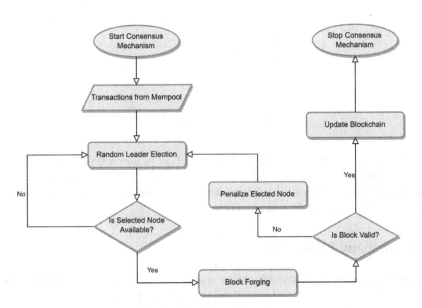

Fig. 1. Algorithmic flow chart

3.2 System Design

The presented data flow diagram (level 2) depicts the system architecture, emphasizing two key users: the leader node and the participant node. Each user is assigned specific tasks within the system. The elected leader node undertakes two primary responsibilities, which encompass block production and distribution. In addition to these, the leader node also performs common tasks such as voting for leader election and transaction

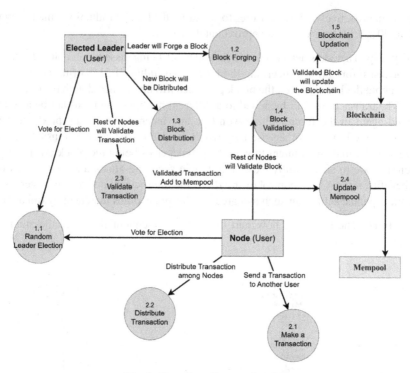

Fig. 2. Data flow diagram (level 2)

validation. Conversely, participant nodes are involved in transaction creation, distribution, and validation of the blocks generated by the leader node. It is important to note that validation mechanisms are implemented at each level of the system to ensure the integrity and accuracy of the processes (Fig. 2).

4   Testing and Evaluation

The primary objective of the testing phase was to ascertain the fulfillment of the anticipated system requirements and uphold the overall quality of the system. Testing standards were established with the purpose of assessing the system and mitigating any discrepancies between the planned system and the actual implementation.

4.1   Degree of Decentralization

The concept of decentralization has been extensively discussed throughout this research project with specific emphasis placed on the potential of the novel consensus protocol to prevent the concentration of power. Given the absence of a suitable metric for assessing the actual degree of decentralization attained by a blockchain system in practice [25], this study has adopted a set of requirements outlined by Gochhayat et al. [26] as a means of testing the decentralized nature of the proposed system.

- The system ought to be designed to operate independently: Individuals possessing a computer and Internet connectivity can establish their own node and partake in the network's activities. The operation of a node necessitates less than 50 MB of memory, rendering the entry threshold negligible in comparison to existing systems (Fig. 3).

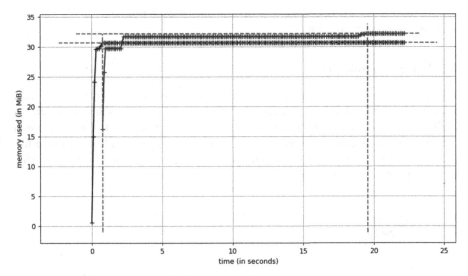

Fig. 3. Runtime memory usage

- Each node is granted the equal privilege to submit transactions to the network: As expounded in the previous chapter, each node possesses transaction functionality.
- Validation of transactions is open to all nodes: Every node within the network validates any transaction it receives before adding it to the mempool. The transaction validation process typically takes less than a millisecond (Fig. 4).

tottime	percall	cumtime	percall	filename:lineno(function)
2.08e-05	2.08e-05	0.0009866	0.0009866	transaction_validation.py:1(<module>)
7.053e-06	7.053e-06	0.0001922	0.0001922	transaction_validation.py:18(Transaction)
7.05e-07	7.05e-07	7.05e-07	7.05e-07	transaction_validation.py:12(TransactionException)

(filtered from 2,365 total entries)

Fig. 4. Time spent on transaction validation

- The equitable distribution of authoritative influence across validating nodes is crucial: One of the key advantages of this proposed system is that each node possesses an equal degree of influence, irrespective of its level of wealth or computational power. This feature fosters true decentralization and eliminates entry barriers.

- It is imperative that the incentive mechanism for operating the Blockchain is equitable: Unlike traditional blockchain systems, the proposed novel blockchain system does not accommodate incentives or block rewards. Instead, it relies on a penalty based mechanism. This unique feature serves to reinforce decentralization and enhance the system's overall security.

Consequently, it can be deduced that the implemented solution possesses the capacity to attain true decentralization.

4.2 Energy Consumption

The primary objective of this research project was to introduce a novel consensus mechanism that could eliminate the concentration of power and accommodate true decentralization. However, it circumvents the need for special hardware and the massive power consumption associated with other consensus mechanisms. The following test results provide an illustration of power consumption while operating a node alongside other supporting applications (Fig. 5).

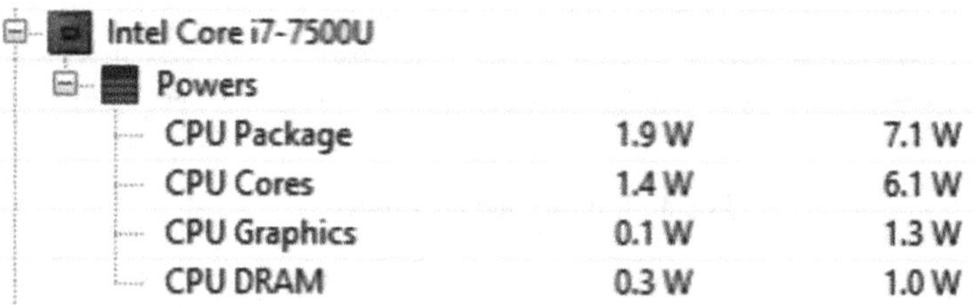

Intel Core i7-7500U		
Powers		
CPU Package	1.9 W	7.1 W
CPU Cores	1.4 W	6.1 W
CPU Graphics	0.1 W	1.3 W
CPU DRAM	0.3 W	1.0 W

Fig. 5. System energy consumption

The observed power usage ranges from 2W to 5W, which stands significantly lower when compared to other consensus mechanisms. Therefore, it can be inferred that the implemented solution effectively mitigates high energy consumption.

4.3 Performance

The performance testing primarily focuses on the core functionality of the implemented novel consensus mechanism which is block production. To test the performance of the block production method proposed in this research project, CPU and Memory profiling is conducted. The profiling is executed on a script that utilizes the 100 pending transactions available on the mempool to generate a block with a difficulty level set to 4 (4 leading zeros) (Fig. 6).

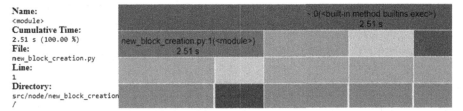

Fig. 6. Time spent on block production

The results of the CPU profiling indicate that the average duration for block production is approximately 2.51 s. It is worth noting that a significant portion of this time (around one-third) is devoted to locating the nonce. The get_nonce() function, in particular, requires 0.795 s to execute (Fig. 7).

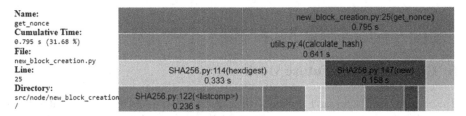

Fig. 7. Time spent on finding nonce

According to the results obtained from memory profiling, the maximum amount of memory utilized during block production has been determined to be less than 50 megabytes. This finding indicates that the process of block production is memory-efficient and does not require a large amount of memory resources. Based on the results obtained from the CPU and memory profiling, it can be concluded that the implemented block production mechanism is fast and highly performant (Fig. 8).

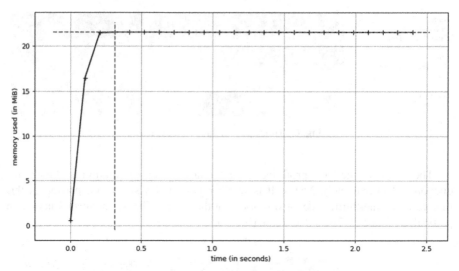

Fig. 8. Memory usage for block production

5   Conclusion and Future Work

The objectives of the research project were successfully achieved by designing, developing, and evaluating a novel consensus protocol that accommodates total decentralization and avoids centralization of power. Additionally, the protocol refrains from utilizing specialized hardware resources and ensures that it does not consume excessive amounts of energy. This can be regarded as a noteworthy contribution to the domain of blockchain. The issue of centralized power in major blockchains has been a topic of discussion over the past decade, but there has been a dearth of studies that specifically examine the degree of decentralization. Given that this project has exhaustively investigated innovative consensus mechanisms that can eradicate centralized power, it can be considered a technological contribution not only to the blockchain domain but also to distributed systems and peer-to-peer networks. An extensive review of the blockchain-related literature, with a focus on the issues present in current blockchains, can also make a significant contribution to scholars interested in the blockchain context.

This research work encompasses several limitations that can be addressed in future endeavors. Firstly, a significant limitation arises from the inability to implement a robust coin distribution mechanism, thereby hindering the effectiveness and applicability of this research project. Secondly, the current project fails to adequately emphasize the security aspect of the blockchain, leading to a noteworthy limitation in terms of its overall scope and depth. Lastly, the absence of scalability achievement within the project constitutes another limitation, highlighting the need for further exploration and development in this area. These limitations collectively underscore the need for future research endeavors to address these shortcomings in order to enhance the overall impact and validity of this study.

Considering the constraints and the novel aspect introduced by this project within the field, numerous prospects for further improvements can be discussed. The primary obstacle in this project, which was the initial allocation of coins, could be viewed as the primary avenue for advancement that needs to be addressed in order to propel the project to the next level. This could involve exploring alternative allocation mechanisms or developing a more efficient and fair distribution strategy. Since security has not been thoroughly addressed in this project, it can be inferred that enhancing the security measures to ensure that the blockchain is not vulnerable to any form of attack would be another significant improvement. This could entail implementing robust encryption algorithms, conducting rigorous penetration testing, and establishing mechanisms for auditing and detecting potential vulnerabilities. Scalability has been a constraint for numerous existing blockchain systems, and the same holds true for this project. Therefore, it is crucial to undertake further investigation into the scalability aspect of blockchain systems, particularly in the context of this project. Furthermore, introducing smart contracts would bring the proposed blockchain into a new realm, thereby making it a significant improvement for the future. This could involve designing and implementing a smart contract platform that allows for the execution of programmable logic within the blockchain, enabling the development of decentralized applications that can leverage the blockchain's security and transparency features. Overall, addressing the issues of initial coin allocation, enhancing security measures, investigating scalability challenges, and incorporating smart contracts would significantly advance the project and contribute to the broader development of blockchain technology.

References

1. Nakamoto, S.: Bitcoin: A Peer-to-Peer Electronic Cash System. 9 (2008)
2. Gamage, H.T.M., Weerasinghe, H.D., Dias, N.G.J.: A Survey on blockchain technology concepts, applications, and issues. SN Comput. Sci. **1**, 114 (2020). https://doi.org/10.1007/s42 979-020-00123-0
3. Kaushal, R.K., Kumar, N., Panda, S.N.: blockchain technology, its applications and open research challenges. J. Phys.: Conf. Ser. **1950**, 012030 (2021). https://doi.org/10.1088/1742-6596/1950/1/012030
4. Praveen, H., Arvindam, S., Pokarna, S.: Thunderbolt: a consensus-based infrastructure for loosely-coupled cluster computing. In: Banerjee, P., Prasanna, V.K., Sinha, B.P. (eds.) HiPC. LNCS, vol. 1745, pp. 61–65. Springer, Heidelberg (1999). https://doi.org/10.1007/978-3-540-46642-0_9
5. Cachin, C., Vukolić, M.: Blockchain Consensus Protocols in the Wild, http://arxiv.org/abs/1707.01873 (2017). https://doi.org/10.48550/arXiv.1707.01873
6. Shrivas, M.K., Yeboah, T., Brunda, S.S.: Hybrid security framework for blockchain platforms. In: 2020 First International Conference on Power, Control and Computing Technologies (ICPC2T), pp. 339–347 (2020). https://doi.org/10.1109/ICPC2T48082.2020.9071477
7. Ren, L.: Proof of Stake Velocity: Building the Social Currency of the Digital Age (2014)
8. Xue, T., Yuan, Y., Ahmed, Z., Moniz, K., Cao, G., Wang, C.: Proof of contribution: a modification of proof of work to increase mining efficiency. In: 2018 IEEE 42nd Annual Computer Software and Applications Conference (COMPSAC), pp. 636–644 (2018). https://doi.org/10.1109/COMPSAC.2018.00096
9. Ferdous, M.S., Chowdhury, M.J.M., Hoque, M.A., Colman, A.: Blockchain consensus algorithms: a survey. http://arxiv.org/abs/2001.07091 (2020)

10. Saad, M., Qin, Z., Ren, K., Nyang, D., Mohaisen, D.: E-PoS: making proof-of-stake decentralized and fair. IEEE Trans. Parallel Distrib. Syst. **32**, 1961–1973 (2021). https://doi.org/10.1109/TPDS.2020.3048853

11. Aluko, O., Kolonin, A.: Proof-of-reputation: an alternative consensus mechanism for blockchain systems. IJNSA. **13**, 23–40 (2021). https://doi.org/10.5121/ijnsa.2021.13403

12. Pang, Y.: A new consensus protocol for blockchain interoperability architecture. IEEE Access. **8**, 153719–153730 (2020). https://doi.org/10.1109/ACCESS.2020.3017549

13. Beikverdi, A., Song, J.: Trend of centralization in Bitcoin's distributed network. In: 2015 IEEE/ACIS 16th International Conference on Software Engineering, Artificial Intelligence, Networking and Parallel/Distributed Computing (SNPD). pp. 1–6 (2015). https://doi.org/10.1109/SNPD.2015.7176229

14. Koch, C., Pieters, G.C.: Blockchain Technology Disrupting Traditional Records Systems (2017). https://papers.ssrn.com/abstract=2997588

15. Shah, B., Shah, N., Shakhla, S., Sawant, V.: Remodeling the healthcare industry by employing blockchain technology. In: 2018 International Conference on Circuits and Systems in Digital Enterprise Technology (ICCSDET), pp. 1–5 (2018). https://doi.org/10.1109/ICCSDET.2018.8821113

16. Szabo, N.: Smart Contracts: Building Blocks for Digital Markets. https://www.fon.hum.uva.nl/rob/Courses/InformationInSpeech/CDROM/Literature/LOTwinterschool2006/szabo.best.vwh.net/smart_contracts_2.html. Accessed 02 May 2023

17. Zheng, Z., Xie, S., Dai, H., Chen, X., Wang, H.: An Overview of Blockchain Technology: Architecture, Consensus, and Future Trends. In: 2017 IEEE International Congress on Big Data (BigData Congress). pp. 557–564 (2017). https://doi.org/10.1109/BigDataCongress.2017.85

18. Tschorsch, F., Scheuermann, B.: Bitcoin and beyond: a technical survey on decentralized digital currencies. IEEE Commun. Surv. Tutor. **18**, 2084–2123 (2016). https://doi.org/10.1109/COMST.2016.2535718

19. Li, C., Palanisamy, B.: Comparison of decentralization in DPoS and PoW blockchains. In: Chen, Z., Cui, L., Palanisamy, B., Zhang, L.-J. (eds.) ICBC 2020. LNCS, vol. 12404, pp. 18–32. Springer, Cham (2020). https://doi.org/10.1007/978-3-030-59638-5_2

20. Oyinloye, D.P., Teh, J.S., Jamil, N., Alawida, M.: Blockchain consensus: an overview of alternative protocols. Symmetry. **13**, 1363 (2021). https://doi.org/10.3390/sym13081363

21. Alzahrani, N., Bulusu, N.: Towards true decentralization: a blockchain consensus protocol based on game theory and randomness. In: Bushnell, L., Poovendran, R., Başar, T. (eds.) GameSec. LNCS, vol. 11199, pp. 465–485. Springer, Cham (2018). https://doi.org/10.1007/978-3-030-01554-1_27

22. De Domenico, M., Baronchelli, A.: The fragility of decentralised trustless socio-technical systems. EPJ Data Sci. **8**, 2 (2019). https://doi.org/10.1140/epjds/s13688-018-0180-6

23. Leonardos, S., Reijsbergen, D., Piliouras, G.: Weighted voting on the blockchain: improving consensus in proof of stake protocols. In: 2019 IEEE International Conference on Blockchain and Cryptocurrency (ICBC), pp. 376–384 (2019). https://doi.org/10.1109/BLOC.2019.8751290

24. Do, T., Nguyen, T., Pham, H.: Delegated proof of reputation: a novel blockchain consensus. In: Proceedings of the 2019 International Electronics Communication Conference, Okinawa Japan, pp. 90–98. ACM (2019). https://doi.org/10.1145/3343147.3343160

25. Wu, K., Peng, B., Xie, H., Huang, Z.: An information entropy method to quantify the degrees of decentralization for blockchain systems. In: 2019 IEEE 9th International Conference on Electronics Information and Emergency Communication (ICEIEC), pp. 1–6 (2019). https://doi.org/10.1109/ICEIEC.2019.8784631

26. Gochhayat, S.P., Shetty, S., Mukkamala, R., Foytik, P., Kamhoua, G.A., Njilla, L.: Measuring decentrality in blockchain based systems. IEEE Access. **8**, 178372–178390 (2020). https://doi.org/10.1109/ACCESS.2020.3026577

Control Plane Comparison of OpenDayLight and Open Network Operating System Controllers

Mohamed Sati⬤, Moad Emshiheet⬤, Ahmed Majouk,
and Salem Omar Sati$^{(\boxtimes)}$⬤

IT Faculty, Misurata University, Misurata, Libya
{m09191148,m09191167,a.almagouk,salem.sati}@it.misuratau.edu.ly

Abstract. Software-Defined Networks (SDN) provide a new networking solution that decouples the control and data planes. The SDN controller as core component of the control plane manages and governs devices in the topology using the OpenFlow signalling protocol. The centralized construction of SDN leads to scalability issues. This paper analysis the number of switches impact on SDN controller performance. The performance metrics considered to measure the control plane quality of SDN controller are Topology Discovery Time (TDT) and Number of Overhead Messages (NOM). The paper focuses on two java based controllers which are OpenDaylight (ODL) and Open Network Operating System (ONOS). The simulation results show that increasing of openFlow switches number impacted on SDN performance of ODL and ONOS. However, the results show that ONOS outperform ODL in terms of performance metrics when the number of switches increases.

Keywords: Controller Scalability · ODL Controller · ONOS Controller · Performance Metrics · Control Plane

1 Introduction

Software-Defined Networks (SDN) [16] is a new networking solution for network management and monitoring via software. Unlike the traditional network architecture, SDN decouples the control plane from the data plane. In SDN, data plane is kept at underlay devices and the control plane is moved up as centralized layer, this layer is in core component termed as a SDN controller. SDN controllers control plane can be deployed to control and monitor the network devices to improve the SDN performance. There are many types of SDN controllers such as, NOX [17] open-source controller which implemented by Nicira. This controller programmed using C++. Where POX [9] also an open-source SDN controller. This controller is inspired from the NOX controller. However, the POX controller is implemented using Python. The other Python controller is RYU [6] controller. On the other side, there are three SDN controllers implemented using Java which are Open Network Operating System (ONOS) [5],

Supported by Misurata University.

OpenDayLight (ODL) [11] and Floodlight [7] controllers. This paper considers a methodology for comparing two java SDN controllers. These SDN controllers are ONOS and ODL controllers. SDN have various protocols which used to communicate between controller and underlay devices such as OpenFlow protocol [12]. This protocol used to generate the control messages between virtual switches and SDN controller. The monitoring and control are the main task of the controller. Where the controller as core component is connected to the virtual switches via a dedicated or shared control channel. The OpenFlow channel between the controller and connected switches is established using a TCP session. Generally the control plane of SDN architecture in large-scale network divided into two main types, the first one is the out-of-band, where the second one is the in-band control plane as showing in Fig. 1 (a) and (b). The out-of- band control plane is the scope of the paper, where the OpenFlow protocol requires a specific control channel between the controller and the virtual switches, which leads to full separation and extra links needed to build this control plane type. However, this out-of-band SDN control plane introduces better scalability compared with in-band control plane. Furthermore, it does not impact by the issues of TCP congestions. Therefore, the overhead messages for out-of-band control plane impact directly by the number of switches and flows, where the number of flows obtained by the number of the virtual switch regardless of SDN controller location.

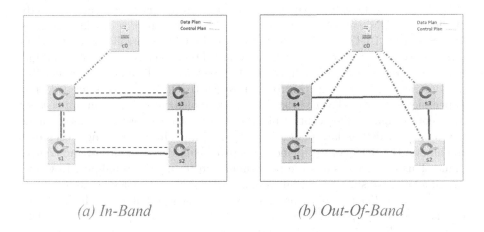

(a) In-Band   (b) Out-Of-Band

Fig. 1. SDN Control plane Types.

The other control plane type of SDN called the in-band as shown in Fig. 1 (a). This type of control plane shares the OpenFlow control message with the user data message at the data plane. Therefore, SDN control and data planes of in-band shares the logical topology of the network. This leads to removing an additional cost for the controller communication with the virtual switches in the topology. This type of control plane is out of the paper scope. Finally this paper compares two SDN controllers. These controllers are ONOS and ODL controllers. The comparison conducted by this paper take into account the IETF RFC 8456 [14]. This comparison of two SDN controllers is in a standalone mode. The comparison done using different topology sizes for measuring specific performance metrics for the out-of-band control plane. The paper layout as follows. Section 2 shows updated related researches of the topic. In Sect. 3, this section demonstrates SDN out-of-band control plane and java controllers. While the evaluation model and performance metric are presented in Sect. 4. Section 5 introduces the simulation configuration and numerical results. Section 6 presents the conclusion and suggests the future work.

2   Related Work

There is a gap of research topics related to the SDN control plane scalability. This paper highlight a deep study and analysis of the out-of-band SDN control plane. Out-of-band control plane is constructed using specific control channel to each switch in the SDN topology, while in-band control plane is constructed using control channels share the data plane connections of SDN. In contrast, in-band SDN control plane constructed based on the network connectivity and data plane links. The paper [13] shows an approach which makes a dedicated control channel when deploying multi protocol for in-band SDN control plane. The approach suggested finds the switches which can deliver through the best paths in the topology. The paper [4] shows a comprehensive comparative study of different SDN controllers. These SDN controllers are java-based named as ONOS and ODL. The paper concludes that the ODL controller is better than the other controller which is ONOS controller. This evaluation done using performance metrics such as throughput and the network traffic load. The paper [15] demonstrates that in-band control in Low Earth Orbit (LEO) is needed. The paper suggests a dual-layer stack. This stack implemented based on upper-layer SDN control plane. This control plane uses a virtual out-of-band control plane based on the existing data plane. The paper [8] introduces a routing mechanism to enhance the SDN control plane. This plane considered as an in-band control plane, This paper measures the performance in terms of throughput. However, the simulations results show that in-band control plane is not scale well in large scale networks. The paper [10] provides an in-band control plane mechanism. The evaluation of the paper with existing approaches shows low performance of data plane forwarding when using in-band control plane. The paper [2] evaluates the performance of open-source Python controllers called POX and RYU controllers. The Mininet emulator is deployed to test both SDN controllers with different topologies. The emulation results show that the RYU controller outperforms the POX controller based on throughput and delay metrics.

3   Out-of-Band SDN Control Plane

The SDN control plane based on OpenFlow control protocol can be classified into two main control plane types. The first control plane is the out-of-band

SDN control plane, where the second type is built using bootstrap and share the data paths of SDN. This control plane called as the in-band control plane. The out-of- band which the scope of this paper, this plane depends on the OpenFlow protocol which requires a dedicated and special control channel. These channels built over TCP session between the controller and virtual switch. Furthermore, The SDN controller used to measure the control plane scalability is deployed in standalone centralized mode, where the distributed domain of the SDN is out of the scope. This paper compares the Out-of-Band control plane of three java based SDN controllers based on number of switches in terms of Topology Discovery Time (TDT) and Number of Overhead Messages (NOM). The SDN controllers considered by the paper and its emulation tool are:-

3.1   OpenDayLight Controller

OpenDaylight is an open-source SDN controller. This controller programmed based on java programming language. ODL controller designed and sported by industry, therefore, it implemented as an industry-standard controller. It acts as a collaborative SDN controller platform for developers and businesses at academy and industry. The OpenFlow protocol basically supported by this controller. This protocol creates an OpenFlow communications over TCP session. It has a south-bound interface, this interface used by controller to communicate as control channel with the topology switches, Moreover, ODL controller supported by large for industry and businesses companies such as CISCO, JUNIPER and HUAWIE as SDN standard. ODL controller supports many SDN control plane protocols such as OpenFlow and NETCONF. This OpenFlow protocol supports modular programming feature. Furthermore, it monitors and controls any topology changes or link failures. ODL supported application at overlay layer can get the information from the underlay layer via northbound API interface, these user space applications can perform efficient analytic approaches. Moreover, these applications distribute different rules over the network topology. ODL controller supports standalone and distributed mode. Where distributed control plane offers high availability and redundancy feature in multi domain SDN topology. The security feature was added to the ODL Lithium release.

3.2   ONOS Controller

The ONOS controller is an other open-source SDN controller. This controller programmed through java programming language for telecommunications and networks. The ONOS controller implemented and target for the distributed SDN control plane. Therefore, it can handles control plane synchronization by deploying the replication. ONOS controller has user friendly online interface. It has also a REST-API for northbound API interface. There are many core objects of ONOS which used to discover topology and collects topology information. ONOS controller discovers network topology as a directed graph topology of uni-direction links. The Northbound and Southbound API interfaces help applications of the user space to communicate and get statistical information from the

ONOS controller. Northbound interface of ONOS controller can be configured in two modes, the first as a fine-grained, where the other mode as an intent-based, therefore, users based on their applications, they can specify their requirements.

3.3   Mininet Emulator

Mininet is a Linux based emulation tool which development for simulating SDN networks. It used in academic research field to emulate a virtual SDN network. It can emulate a virtual switch in kernel or user space. The next generation of cloud and data centers should be manageable, programmable and scalable. Therefore, researchers implementing the best solutions to eliminate the issues of the traditional network infrastructure. Industry and academic researchers test their experimental scenarios using the common SDN emulator which is the Mininet emulator. Mininet emulator enables the researchers to test a different virtual switches and SDN controllers using different topologies. Mininet virtual switches support OpenFlow and other control protocols in kernel or user spaces. Mininet with other tools, it can calculate the network QoS and performance metrics such as bandwidth, overhead and delay. Mininet emulator can simulation multiple controllers as distributed control plane. It enabling the researcher to test a multi domain of SDN architecture. This is helpful for researchers when simulating the various topologies using different SDN controllers. The Mininet command line provides easy way to emulate a virtual switches with controllers of different SDN topology. Mininet emulator has different network features. It can simulate a complex and large-scale networks. Mininet emulator is a superior emulator of SDN architecture compared to existing virtualisation tools.

4   Evaluation Model and Metrics

The comparison of two java-based SDN controllers based on RFC 8456 is conducted by using the following network model and metrics:-

4.1   Network Topology and Scenarios

The topology form determines the control plane type of SDN. The connections between controller and topology switches determine the control plane type. Also the number of switches related to the controllers mode. Where the control plane completes its discovery process at the end of convergence time. The convergence time is completed when the controller discovers all topology switches, Then controller reaches to the fully stable state. The convergence time or TDT depends on the number of virtual switches in the topology and the type of control plane. Obviously, the convergence time depends on the control plane weather it in-band or out-of-band control plane. This paper focuses on the control plane scalability and performance of ONOS and ODL controllers based on network topology size [1,3]. It considers the following network topology forms.

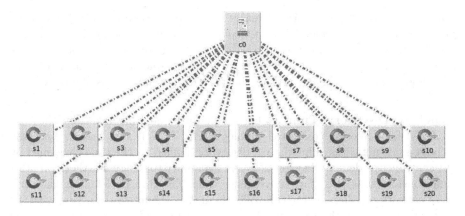

Fig. 2. Out-of-Band Scalability Topology.

The comparison of ONOS and ODL control plane is conducted using the topology of scalability. This topology consist of number of virtual switches connected to standalone controller. The control plane of this topology is an out-of-band control plane. This topology as shown in Fig. 2 is considered as test for control plane scalability, where the number of connected virtual switches increased from 10 to 70 switches. The dedicated channel capacity of SDN out-of-band control plane depends on the maximum number of connected switches. This measurement is considered based on the test scenario of scalability in RFC 8456. The topology of unconnected switches as shown in Fig. 2 applied to evaluate the SDN out-of-band control plane performance using ODL and ONOS controllers. This topology has no connections between switches, where all switches in the topology connected with standalone controller via out-of-band control plane. Furthermore, the number of switches impact on the performance of southbound interface of the controller. The number of dedicated control plane channel in the topology impact by the number of the switches attached to the SDN controller. Furthermore, for measuring control plane scalability of ONOS and ODL. The out-of-band control plane of the topology has no data plane connectivity or any links between switches.

4.2   Performance Metrics

The types of quantitative performance metrics for evaluating out-of-band control plane of SDN controllers include the following:-

Number of Overhead Messages (NOM). This metric used to count the control plane traffic of OpenFlow. The amount of control plane messages which is sent between the controller and virtual switches are measured and compared based on out-of-band control plane type. The amount of sent/received OpenFlow messages of the ODL and ONOS controllers calculated based on scalability topology. It is obvious that this topology has no data connectivity between switches.

Furthermore, the topology size increases based on the number of switches using Out-of-Band control plane. The control plane messages is generated only without the data plane packets traversed through the topology in the out-of-band control plane. The ratio of control plane messages to data plane data is zero. As the size of topology increases, the growth of control messages number is observed.

Topology Discovery Time (TDT). Measure the time taken by the controller(s) for detecting connected topology. The TDT is very criteria specially in large-scale networks. This time of discovery defined by the time consumed by the controller to detect all switches in the scalability topology. Furthermore, this time considered as cold start convergence time. The time of detecting the complete network topology by the controller defined as the interval starting with the first switch discovery by the controller at its southbound interface to the ending time of discovering the last switch in scalability topology. This time of TDT impact by the topology size based on the number of switches in the topology. This time impact also on end-to-end delay which is QoS and criteria for different SDN applications.

5   Simulation and Numerical Results

The comparison between ODL and ONOS controllers is conducted through the Mininet emulator. The comparison considers scalability topology which depends on topology size for both controllers. The comparison is based on the RFC 8456. The comparison was based on the number of switches in terms of TDT and NOM performance metrics. The comparison of both java controllers focusing on the out-of-band control plane with single controller standalone topology. The control plane scalability comparison was based on the OpenFlow protocol and un-connected kernel space virtual switches. The control plane for all topologies was based on dedicated control channels with no data plane connectivity between switches. The topology size was changed based on the number of switches from 20 to 70 switches for both controllers. The comparison between ODL and ONOS controllers with different scalability topologies as configuration shown in the Table 1.

The TDT measured using Python tool which finds the time interval between detecting the first switch to the time when finding the last switch in the topology. This time may be defined as topology cold start convergence time. The switches connected with controllers with OpenFlow protocol version 1.0. For creation of different topology size the MiniEdit GUI tool is deployed to create these topologies. Using this MiniEdit, different network topology size were created for emulation in the Mininet emulation tool, these topologies are used to compare between ODL and ONOS controllers. Wireshark, and Python topology discovery tool (TDT) are used to compare the tested controllers (ONOS and ODL). The scalability topology of standalone controller is used as model to compare the ODL and ONOS controllers. This comparison applied for both controllers using the same configuration to grantee precise comparison results. After the creation

Table 1. Mininet Emulator Settings.

No	Settings	Value(s)
1	Connection Type	Fast Ethernet
2	Number of Switches	From 20 to 70 step 10
3	Link Delay	10 ms
4	Topologies	Switched connected to controller via Out-of-Band Control plane
5	SDN Controllers	ODL and ONOS
6	Controllers Programming Language	Java
7	Control Channel	Dedicated
8	IP	Version 4
9	Controllers Versions	ODL 0.8.4 ONOS 1.12
10	Metrics	Number of Overhead Messages - NOM Topology Discovery Time - TDT

of different network topology sizes, each topology applied on each controller and results collected by calculating the main performance's QoS parameters such as TDT and NOM. These metrics selected because they are the main two metrics which evaluate the control plane for network system. The following subsections demonstrates the collected results for each metric of TDT and NOM. The ONOS and ODL controllers results are collected and compared in terms of discovery time and overhead messages count.

5.1 Number of Overhead Messages (NOM)

The standalone topology mode has many control messages. These control messages are exchanged between virtual switches and SDN controller. These messages are exchanged for topology discovery and OpnFlow control negotiation based on out-of-band control plane. The TCP connection will establish between the virtual switch and SDN controller to create the dedicated control channel. When the TCP session three way hand shaking process is completed, the switch will a accomplish TCP connection with the standalone controller. The Open-Flow control messages are exchanged through the out-of-band control plane. The OpenFlow protocol initiates an OpenFlow control plane session by sending a Hello control message to the SDN controller. When the standalone controller receipt of this Hello message, the SDN controller replies with its OpenFlow Hello message. The standalone controller then sends an other OpenFlow control message called feature request message. When the switch receipt of this feature request control message, the virtual switch sends an other OpenFlow message termed as a feature reply message to the standalone controller. The standalone controller receives the OpenFlow message of feature reply and it starts an OpenFlow session with the specific virtual switch. The feature reply message sent by the switch includes all switch attributes/parameters. These attributes/parameters including the physical address and other parameters of

OpenFlow protocol. The standalone controller adds the physical address as the switch ID in its topology information.

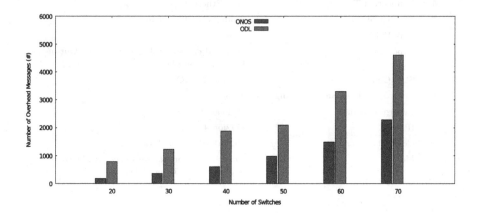

Fig. 3. Number of Overhead Messages of ONOS and ODL.

The standalone controller must identify how the virtual switch is connected to the controller via control channel. To specify this, the standalone controller sends a control message called a probe message to the specific switch. When the switch receives this OpenFlow control message, the switch assumes this control message as unknown traffic and sends this back to the controller as a Packet-In message. Then the controller receives the Packet-In and it generates an OpenFlow Packet-Out control message. The comparison between two java controllers of SDN which are ODL and ONOS considers mentioned OpenFlow control messages. These control messages for topology discovery and OpenFlow communication between virtual switch and standalone controller. This Number of Overhead Messages (NOM) metric counts all generated OpenFlow messages of out-of-ban control plane of both ODL and ONOS controllers. Figure 3 shows that the Number of Overhead Messages (NOM). These messages are exchanged between ODL and ONOS controllers with connected topology switch of 20 to 70 switches. As Fig. 3 demonstrates that ONOS controller topology has the lowest overhead control messages compared with ODL controller in different topology sizes from 20 to 70 switches. This is because ONOS controller eliminates some of control messages and supports distributed SDN domain and control plane. Figure 3 shows that ONOS has the lower overhead messages in all sizes, and the difference between them grows as the number of switches increases.

5.2 Topology Discovery Time (TDT)

The Topology Discovery Time (TDT) metric is very important factor for different topology sizes of different network types. This time considered as a network convergence time which is defined in SDN as the time spent by the SDN controller to detect all virtual switches of the topology. At the end of this time the network topology will be in passive state in which all virtual switches have dedicated control channel with SDN controller. Alternatively, in SDN, convergence time can be defined as the time spent until all switches of SDN out-of-band control plane are connected with SDN controller via southbound interface. The TDT is determined by custom tool based on the Python programming language. The topology size was changed from 20 to 70 switches to discover the impact of topology size on the performance of out-of-band control plane. The topology size changed for both ODL and ONOS controllers. For all scenarios which applied on ODL and ONOS controllers there is no any data connectivity between switches. The tool used to calculate TDT metric. This tool is better than ping utility where ping used for in-band control plane. But in this paper simulation scenarios of out-of-band control plane, there is a need to detect the topology without data plane. Therefore, the implemented tool calculates the TDT metric for both ODL and ONOS controllers. The TDT tool communicates with the ODL or ONOS controller to detect the connected virtual switches in the topology. When the user deploy this tool to calculate the TDT metric. The user should specify the controller type and the maximum number of switches in the tested topology. If the current number collected by the tool is zero. This means that the mininet emulator is not connected yet with SDN controller. The user should run the controller, then the tool starts the test and stores the current time in milliseconds, then the tool waits the user to connect the mininet topology with the controller.

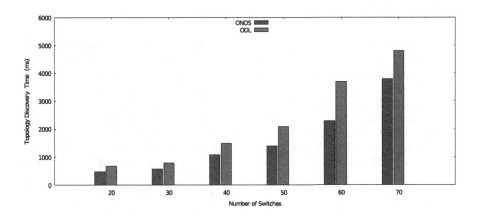

Fig. 4. Topology Discovery Time of ONOS and ODL.

When the topology connected the first switch with controller, the TDT starts until the controller detect the last switch which specified by the user input as maximum number of switches in the tested topology. Current number of switches reaches the total number of switches that have been specified by the user. Then the tool stores the time of detecting last switches in milliseconds.

Finally the tool determines the TDT by subtracts the last switch detecting time from the first detected switch time to calculate the TDT in milliseconds. From Fig. 4, it can observed that the ONOS has low TDT when compared with ODL controller. Furthermore, ONOS has a low TDT time when compared with the ODL controller regardless the topology size. This is because ONOS is considered the multi-domain SDN controller. The scalability topology of 70 switches has the highest TDT time. This is because the SDN out-of-band control plane impacts by the number of OpenFlow sessions with controller. In term of TDT, it shows that ONOS has the lower TDT, but the variation in results are not linear, in the scenario of the 60 switches it can observer that TDT of ODL is spikes.

6   Conclusion and Future Work

This paper compares between ODL and ONOS controllers based on a different topology size using the network metrics such as NOH and TDT. Comparison results conducted by the Mininet emulator. The paper also taking into the account the topology size based on the number of switches, The control plane considered by this paper is out-of-band control plane. The results show that ONOS a superiority when compared with the ODL controller in terms of TDT and NOM metrics. In future work, more controllers such as Floodlight controller maybe investigated using other metrics to have deep investigation of SDN control plane performance and scalability measurement.

References

1. Alatersh, F.M., Sati, S., Sullabi, M.: Impact of network topologies on RPL performance. In: 22nd International Arab Conference on Information Technology, ACIT 2021, Muscat, Oman, 21–23 December 2021, pp. 1–7. IEEE (2021)
2. Alzarog, J., Almhishi, A., Alsunousi, A., Abulifa, T.A., Eltarjaman, W., Sati, S.O.: Pox controller evaluation based on tree topology for data centers. In: 2022 International Conference on Data Analytics for Business and Industry (ICDABI), pp. 67–71 (2022). https://doi.org/10.1109/ICDABI56818.2022.10041622
3. Alzarog, J., Almhishi, A., Alsunousi, A., Elasaifer, A., Eltarjaman, W., Sati, S.O.: SDN controllers comparison based on network topology. In: 2022 Workshop on Microwave Theory and Techniques in Wireless Communications (MTTW), pp. 204–209 (2022). https://doi.org/10.1109/MTTW56973.2022.9942565
4. Badotra, S., Panda, S.N.: Evaluation and comparison of OpenDayLight and open networking operating system in software-defined networking. Clust. Comput. **23**(2), 1281–1291 (2020)
5. Berde, P., et al.: ONOS: towards an open, distributed SDN OS. In: Akella, A., Greenberg, A.G. (eds.) Proceedings of the Third Workshop on Hot Topics in Software Defined Networking, HotSDN 2014, Chicago, Illinois, USA, August 22, 2014, pp. 1–6. ACM (2014)
6. Bhardwaj, S., Panda, S.N.: Performance evaluation using RYU SDN controller in software-defined networking environment. Wirel. Pers. Commun. **122**(1), 701–723 (2022)

7. Chen, X., Guo, D., Ma, W., He, L.: FloodSight: a visual-aided floodlight controller extension for SDN networks. In: Chen, Y., Christie, M., Tan, W. (eds.) SG 2015. LNCS, vol. 9317, pp. 75–86. Springer, Cham (2017). https://doi.org/10.1007/978-3-319-53838-9_6

8. Fan, W., Yang, F.: Centralized trust-based in-band control for SDN control channel. IEEE Access **8**, 4289–4300 (2020)

9. Jmal, R., Fourati, L.C.: Implementing shortest path routing mechanism using OpenFlow POX controller. In: The International Symposium on Networks, Computers and Communications, ISNCC 2014, Hammamet, Tunisia, June 17–19, 2014, pp. 1–6. IEEE (2014)

10. Kumazoe, K., Shibata, M., Tsuru, M.: A P4 BMv2-based feasibility study on a dynamic in-band control channel for SDN. In: Barolli, L., Miwa, H. (eds.) Advances in Intelligent Networking and Collaborative Systems. INCoS 2022. LNNS, vol. 527. Springer, Cham (2022). https://doi.org/10.1007/978-3-031-14627-5_45

11. Medved, J., Varga, R., Tkacik, A., Gray, K.: OpenDayLight: towards a model-driven SDN controller architecture. In: Proceeding of IEEE International Symposium on a World of Wireless, Mobile and Multimedia Networks, WoWMoM 2014, Sydney, Australia, 19 June 2014, pp. 1–6. IEEE Computer Society (2014)

12. Narisetty, R., et al.: OpenFlow configuration protocol: implementation for the of management plane. In: 2013 Second GENI Research and Educational Experiment Workshop, Salt Lake City, UT, USA, 20–22 March 2013, pp. 66–67. IEEE Computer Society (2013)

13. Raza, A., Lee, S.: Gate switch selection for in-band controlling in software defined networking. IEEE Access **7**, 5671–5681 (2019)

14. Vengainathan, B., Basil, A., Tassinari, M., Manral, V., Banks, S.: Benchmarking methodology for software-defined networking (SDN) controller performance. RFC **8456**, 1–64 (2018)

15. Wang, N., Dong, C., Liu, L., Mian, W., Liang, B.: An SDN based highly reliable in-band control framework for LEO mega-constellations. In: 6th IEEE International Conference on Computer and Communication Systems, ICCCS 2021, Chengdu, China, 23–26 April 2021, pp. 970–975. IEEE (2021)

16. Xu, F., He, J., Wu, X.: First study on supply and demand network with multi-functional and opening characteristics for enterprise (SDN). In: Proceedings of the IEEE International Conference on Systems, Man & Cybernetics: The Hague, Netherlands, 10–13 October 2004, pp. 2108–2113. IEEE (2004)

17. Yao, G., Bi, J., Xiao, P.: Source address validation solution with OpenFlow/NOX architecture. In: Proceedings of the 19th annual IEEE International Conference on Network Protocols, ICNP 2011, Vancouver, BC, Canada, 17–20 October 2011, pp. 7–12. IEEE Computer Society (2011)

SRISC: Open Source Soft Processor Side Channel Analysis Attack Framework Using RISC-V

Darshana Jayasinghe[✉] and Sri Parameswaran

School of Electrical and Computer Engineering, The University of Sydney, Sydney, NSW 2006, Australia
{Darshana.jayasinghe,Sri.parameswaran}@Sydney.edu.au

Abstract. Side channel analysis (SCA) attacks on soft processor systems (such as RISC-V and LEON3) are typically performed on FPGA prototyping boards. For the first time, this paper presents a RISC-V-based soft processor SCA framework (referred to as *SRISC*) to perform power-based, electromagnetic radiation-based and execution time-based SCA attacks against cryptographic algorithms and to test countermeasures on soft processor systems. The proposed *SRISC* framework is demonstrated on a commercial side-channel analysis attack board, SASEBO-GIII (referred to as *SRISC*-SASEBO). *SRISC* consists of hardware modules to calculate cryptographic operations using hardware circuits.

As a case study to test the implementation of a countermeasure, a balanced AES countermeasure is discussed to show the effectiveness of building hybrid countermeasures (which use both hardware and software components–hardware/software co-design) to reduce the information leakage to mitigate power analysis attacks. The software implementation of the balanced AES countermeasure revealed 14 bytes (of 16 bytes) of the secret key in 18,000 encryptions. The balanced hybrid AES countermeasure revealed only eight bytes (of 16 bytes) of the secret key for the same number of encryptions making software-hardware co-design countermeasures more promising to mitigate power analysis attack vulnerabilities.

Keywords: Power Analysis Attacks · RISC-V · SASEBO FPGA

1 Introduction

SCA attacks use the byproducts of the execution of cryptographic implementations, such as power dissipation (referred to as power analysis attacks [20]), electromagnetic radiation (referred to as EM attacks [2]), cache hit/miss information (referred to as cache timing attacks [6]), elapsed time (referred to as timing attacks [19]) and fault attacks [18]. This paper limits the focus to power, EM and timing attacks.

© The Author(s), under exclusive license to Springer Nature Switzerland AG 2024
D. Herath et al. (Eds.): APANConf 2023, CCIS 1995, pp. 112–124, 2024.
https://doi.org/10.1007/978-3-031-51135-6_10

Soft processor systems are widely used due to the ability to modify the hardware specifications by the designer and are often implemented on FPGAs. MicroBlaze, PicoBlaze, NIOS II are examples of commercial soft processor systems, and LEON 3, OpenRISC and LowRISC are examples of open source soft processor systems. LowRISC is based on RISC-V open source ISA [4].

The open source soft processor systems are widely used since designers can change the internal architecture of the processor (e.g. Arithmetic Logic Unit–ALU) and the hardware designs compared to a commercial soft processor system (e.g. the source code of Xilinx MicroBlaze soft processor is an intellectual property of Xilinx and cannot be modified by the hardware designer). Therefore, open-source soft processor systems enable the development of new countermeasures which cannot be tested using commercial soft processors (e.g. masking the ALU). SCA attacks on soft processors are typically conducted on general-purpose FPGA prototyping boards [15].

This paper, for the first time, proposes an open source SCA attack framework (referred to as *SRISC*) which is based on LowRISC RISC-V soft processor system [22] to test both software-based countermeasures and hardware-based countermeasures. *SRISC* is implemented on a commercial side-channel analysis attack board (SASEBO GIII board [21]) and referred to as *SRISC*-SASEBO, which has enough resources to hold both complete RISC-V soft processor system and countermeasures (source code and example projects can be found on [1]). *SRISC* consists of hardware modules to calculate cryptographic operations using hardware circuits while the main cryptographic algorithm is running on the RISC-V core to reduce information leakage.

1.1 Contributions

- We present a RISC-V soft processor-based (open source) SCA attack framework to evaluate both software and hardware-based countermeasures against power attacks, EM attacks and timing attacks.
- As a case study, we demonstrate a hybrid AES balancing countermeasure implementation which uses both hardware and software components to calculate AES ciphertext and demonstrates that it leaks less information (needs a large number of power traces to reveal the secret key) compared to the software implementation of the identical countermeasure.

The rest of the paper is organised as follows. The Sect. 2 describes the power, EM and timing attacks on soft processor systems and previously proposed soft processor systems. The Sect. 3 provides the necessary background to understand the LowRISC soft processor systems, SASEBO GIII FPGA board, CPA attacks, and the AES algorithm, briefly. The Sect. 4 presents the architecture of the proposed *SRISC* soft processor SCA attack framework. The Sect. 5 presents the balanced AES implementation to demonstrate the information leakage of the implemented hybrid countermeasure (hardware/software co-design). The experimental setup is explained in the Sect. 6. The results are presented and discussed in the Sect. 7. The discussion is presented in the Sect. 8 and the paper is concluded in the Sect. 9.

2 Related Work

This section describes previously proposed SCA attacks and countermeasures on soft processor systems and soft processor system SCA frameworks. Mane et al. [24] proposed a balanced AES implementation using Altera Nios II soft processor system on an Altera DE 2 FPGA prototyping board. Barte et al. [5] proposed a masked soft processor core (similar to MicroBlaze) on a Xilinx Spartan 3 FPGA prototyping board. Tillich et al. [27] proposed a masked countermeasure for Leon3 soft processor system on a Xilinx ML410 FPGA prototyping board. Note that none of the aforementioned countermeasures rely on the architecture of the soft processor system to achieve security and were built by modifying the hardware components of the soft processor core/system.

Arsath et al. [26] proposed a framework to measure SCA leakages in RISC-V processors using simulated Value Change Dump (VCD) files to quantise power dissipation of different components of RISC-V core. Side channel analysis attacks on soft processor systems were limited to developing countermeasures on soft processor systems. A hardware masking-based countermeasure for RISC-V core ALU was proposed by Gross et al. [16] to hide the information being processed. Outside of the ALU (e.g., memory bus and peripheral bus), the information is unmasked. Similar to [16], the authors in [11] proposed a masked RISC-V ALU on a Xilinx Zynq FPGA prototyping board [12].

Compared to [5,11,16,24,26,27], *SRISC* is a framework which allows for differing countermeasures to be tested. *SRISC* SCA attack framework is open-source. Compared to the Arsath et al. [26], *SRISC*-SASEBO is demonstrated on a hardware SCA attack board and *SRISC*-SASEBO can be used to check EM attack and timing attack vulnerabilities. Compared to [16] and [11], *SRISC* SCA framework is a complete RISC-V soft processor system.

To the best of our knowledge, this is the first open-source soft processor system framework proposed to perform SCA attacks. The source code of *SRISC* can be found in [1].

3 Background

This section briefly explains RISC-V ISA and LowRISC soft processor system, SASEBO GIII, AES and CPA attacks.

3.1 RISC-V Instruction Set Architecture–ISA and LowRISC Soft Processor System

RISC-V is an open source Instruction Set Architecture (ISA) which is used by most prominent technology companies, such as Google, Western Digital, NVIDIA, etc. [14]. LowRISC is a soft processor system implementation of the 64-bit RISC-V ISA (based on Rocket chip core which was implemented by the University of California, Berkeley [4]) and uses NASTI bus (similar to Xilinx AXI bus) to connect hardware components. We used version 0.2 of LowRISC in this paper to implement *SRISC* side-channel analysis attack framework. LowRISC uses both Dynamic Random Access Memory (DRAM) and BlockRAM (BRAM) in the FPGA to store data and instructions.

3.2 Side Channel Analysis Attack Board - SASEBO GIII

SASEBO GIII board is specially manufactured for power, EM and fault-based attacks and contains filters to isolate of noise from the power lines to measure the aforementioned side-channel leakages. SASEBO GIII contains two FPGAs: a cryptographic FPGA on which the cryptographic algorithm implementation is programmed, and a control FPGA which bridges the data path between the computer and cryptographic FPGA to send and receive plaintexts and cipher-texts.

3.3 Advanced Encryption Standard (AES)

AES is the most widely used block cipher. The size of the input (referred to as plaintext) and output (referred to as ciphertext) are 128-bits. AES has four steps: SubByte, ShiftRow, MixColumn and AddRoundKey, in each round.

In the software implementation of AES, the SubByte operation is precalculated and stored as a table lookup (referred to as Sbox) or the SubByte operation and the MixColumn operation are precalculated as table lookups (referred to as T-tables) to speed up the encryption [6]. In the hardware implementation of AES, The SubByte operation can be precalculated and stored as hardware table lookups or calculated using dedicated circuits [9]. Both Sbox table lookups-based AES implementations and T-table based AES implementations can be executed on soft processors. Based on the ability to change the hardware components of the soft processor system, hardware Sbox circuits can also be integrated into the soft processor systems to execute AES.

3.4 Correlation Power Analysis (CPA) Attacks

CPA attacks belong to Differential Power Analysis (DPA) attacks where hypo-thetical power dissipation is calculated based on either plaintext or ciphertext with a guessed secret key (or round key). The hypothetical power dissipation calculation is approximated with the number of bit transitions (referred to as Hamming distance) or the number of 1 s (referred to as Hamming weight) in the hypothetical value calculated for a cryptographic algorithm [25]. The actual power dissipation is correlated with the hypothetical power dissipation to find the secret key. As an example, software implementations of AES are often attacked using the hypothetical power dissipation of the output of Sbox table lookup or T-table lookup. Once the Hamming distance or weight values are calculated, the Pearson Correlation Coefficient algorithm is used to calculate the ranking of the hypothetical power dissipation with the actual power consumption of the cryptographic algorithm. Readers are advised to refer [7,17,25] regarding CPA attacks on AES.

4 *SRISC*: RISC-V Soft Processor Framework

This section describes the *SRISC* SCA attack framework which is built based on LowRISC RISC-V soft processor system and *SRISC*-SASEBO implementation. *SRISC* SCA framework consists of a Rocket chip RISC-V core and a NASTI interconnect (crossbar) which connects data and instruction memory with input/output peripherals and custom hardware modules as shown in Fig. 1. Both memory channel and I/O channel are connected to the RISC-V core using NASTI bus [22] (or AXI bus) and NASTI interconnect (Similar to AXI Interconnect [31]). The memory channel is divided into two sections: DRAM (can be either DDR3 RAM or DDR2 RAM) and BlockRAM [30]. The size of the DRAM is limited by the number of DRAM chips available and the capacity of each DRAM chip. The total size of BlockRAM is limited by the number of BlockRAM modules available in the FPGA (RAMB36E1 modules [30]). The DRAM stores the bootloader, such as Berkley Boot Loader (BBL) [23], to boot soft processor system using the Linux operating system and store the large data structures in the bare metal mode (without an operating system) in LowRISC.

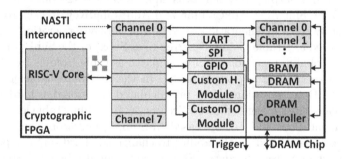

Fig. 1. Architecture of *SRISC*.

The NASTI interconnect can connect up to eight input/output peripherals such as Universal Asynchronous Receiver/Transmitter (UART), Serial Peripheral Interface (SPI) and custom hardware modules such as data transfer modules and special hardware circuits to perform cryptographic operations or precalculated table lookups (such as AES Sbox or T-tables) and hardware monitors to probe data packets communicating through the NASTI bus. Two unused NASTI interconnect ports are left to make expansions possible for users in *SRISC*.

The clock distribution of the *SRISC* is shown in Fig. 2a. The DDR memory controller (generated from Xilinx Memory Interface Generator–MIG) is a Xilinx IP that implements the DDR RAM protocols and interfaces DRAM chip(s) with the processor data bus. It also has an integrated Xilinx clock manager (Mixed-Mode Clock Manager–MMCM) to generate the system clock to drive the Rocket chip and other peripherals. Thus, the four unused clock outputs of the clock manager can be utilised to supply the clock to different clock domains (e.g. running a UART module from an external clock).

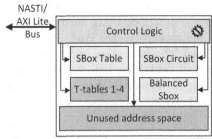

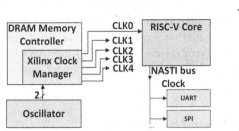

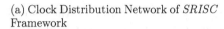

(a) Clock Distribution Network of *SRISC* Framework

(b) Custom Hardware Module to Perform AES Cryptographic Operations of *S-RISC*

Fig. 2. SRISC Clock Network and Custom Hardware Module Architecture.

4.1   Communication with the Computer

In a typical power analysis attack, an EM attack or a timing attack, plaintexts are sent from a computer (such as a PC) or an embedded device; and ciphertexts are received from the cryptographic implementation.

The data communication with the computer is established either using Custom IO module or Xilinx UART module. The SPI module communicates with either a Secure Digital (SD) card or a micro SD card breakout board to load the operating system. The oscilloscope or the Analog to Digital Converter (ADC) to collect the power and EM leakages are triggered by using a General Purpose Input Output module (GPIO).

4.2   Custom Hardware Modules

LowRISC soft processor system allows custom hardware modules built by users to be connected to the RISC-V core. In *SRISC*, a custom hardware module is added as an example to calculate cryptographic operations using hardware circuits or store precalculated operations as lookup tables using hardware circuits to implement hybrid countermeasures which use software/hardware. As an example, Sbox table lookups can be stored on the FPGA as hardware lookup tables (referred to as LUTs [30]) and the input to the table lookup and the output of the table lookup can be referred via addressable registers. In a similar manner, hardware circuits can be used to calculate the operations on the fly. This is helpful to calculate SubByte operations on the fly using hardware circuits (in contrast to precalculated Sbox lookup tables) for AES, store balanced Sbox table lookups (Hamming weight of Sbox table lookups are balanced to achieve input independent power dissipation as explained in the Sect. 3.4) and masked SubByte operations to mitigate side channel analysis attacks. This is paramount in developing hardware modules for the software implementations which have significant overheads.

In *SRISC*, we have integrated Sbox table lookups, T-table lookups and Sub-Byte operations using hardware circuits and a Hamming weight balanced Sbox table lookups in the custom hardware module as shown in the Fig. 2b. Additional 32 addressable registers are left for further expansions (if 32 additional spaces are not enough, hardware designers can create new NASTI-lite/AXI-lite component with higher address range as explained in [13]) to connect custom hardware components.

4.3   Measuring Clock Cycles for Timing Side Channels

In order to test timing attack or cache timing attack vulnerabilities, the elapsed time of the cryptographic operation should be measured with high precision counters (typically using cycle-accurate hardware counters [10]). *SRISC* uses **rdcycle** instruction of RISC-V core to calculate elapsed time of cryptographic implementations.

Cache timing attack success depends on the cache associativity, cache replacement policy and size of caches [29]. RISC-V core has two levels of caches: level 1(L1) and level 2(L2). The size of each cache and associativity of the RISC-V core and how to change the cache sizes are explained in [4, 8].

4.4   SRISC Framework on SASEBO GIII (SRISC-SASEBO)

The communication with the computer in *SRISC*-SASEBO is achieved via the control FPGA interconnect with the cryptographic FPGA of SASEBO GIII and implementing data and control protocol in the Custom IO module (referred to as SASEBO IO) of *SRISC*. The SASEBO IO module sends and receives data from the control FPGA of SASEBO GIII as explained in the Sect. 3.2. The SASEBO IO module enables users to deploy data collection programs and verification programs provided with SASEBO GIII [21]. The first pin of the SASEBO GIII GPIO connector port is used to trigger the oscilloscope. *SRISC* SCA framework is portable and does not depend on any inbuilt hardware components of the SASEBO GIII board.

5   Case Study: Balanced AES Implementation Using Hardware/Software Co-design

In this Section, we discuss a balanced AES implementation in which Sbox lookup tables are stored in the custom hardware module discussed in the Sect. 4.2 and the rest of the operations are calculated on the RISC-V core.

Balancing countermeasures on soft/hard processors work by processing both data and complement of data to balance the number of 1 s and 0 s in processing in the ALU. We implemented an AES software implementation with a balanced hamming weight (similar to [28]) where the number of 1 s and 0 s in the inputs and outputs of each operation are constant (eight 1 s and eight 0 s to be precise) irrespective of the information being processed in the cryptographic implementation as a case study to compare the information leakage.

We implemented two Hamming weight balanced AES (similar to [3]) implementations: balanced Sbox lookup tables are stored in the source code (stored as an array in the software code) and in the custom hardware module which also resets the data and address buses to 0 (similar to precharge in [28]). Hamming weight balanced ShiftRow, MixColumn and RoundKey operations are performed on the soft processor core. (detailed architecture is omitted due to the space restriction).

6   Experimental Setup

We implemented *SRISC*-SASEBO on a SASEBO GIII board which contains a Xilinx Kintex-7 325T FPGA as the cryptographic FPGA. The SCA attacks were carried out on a bare metal (i.e., without an operating system). The RISC-V core (Rocket chip) in *SRISC*-SASEBO framework was generated and synthesized using the information provided in [22]. The Bitstream with the executables to run cryptographic algorithms was generated using the instructions provided in [1]. The clock of the RISC-V core was set at 50MHz.

We used the SASEBO IO module (explained in the Sect. 4.2) in *SRISC*-SASEBO to send plaintexts to the cryptographic algorithm and receive the ciphertext from the computer (e.g. PC).

Five unprotected AES implementations are tested on *SRISC* framework to compare the SCA attack leakages: AES implementations using Software Sbox lookup tables (referred to as **SboxSW**), hardware Sbox lookup table (referred to as **SboxHW**), Software T-table lookup (referred to as **T-tableSW**), hardware T-table lookup (referred to as **T-tableHW**) and hardware circuit to calculate SubByte operation (referred to as **SubByteGen**). A Hamming weight-balanced software Sbox lookup table (referred to as **BalSboxSW**) and a Hamming weight-balanced hardware Sbox lookup table (referred to as **BalSboxHW**) based protected AES implementations are constructed to test the information leakage of Hamming weight balanced AES operations.

Power and EM information leakages are measured using an Agilent DSOX 2012A oscilloscope with an Aaronia UBBV1 signal amplifier (as shown in Fig. 3).

CPA attacks are carried out using NVIDIA Tesla P100 Graphic Processing Units (GPUs) on different AES implementations running on *SRISC*-SASEBO. Each CPA attack is repeated 100 times to calculate the success rates which provides an average number of power traces to reveal the complete secret key or individual key bytes of the secret key from the particular AES implementation.

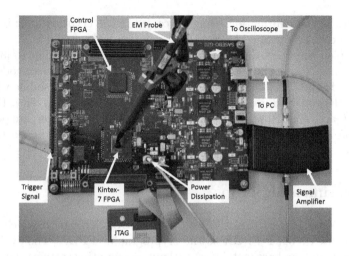

Fig. 3. Power and EM Attack Experimental Setup on SASEBO GIII.

7   Results

This section presents SCA attack results obtained for *SRISC* SCA framework
SRISC-SASEBO. CPA attack results for power analysis attacks are shown in the
Fig. 4-(A). According to the Fig. 4-(A), **SboxSW** AES implementation reveals
the secret key in around 1700 encryptions, and **SboxHW** reveals the secret key
in around 900 encryptions. **T-tableSW** and **T-tableHW** AES implementations
reveal secret keys in around 450 encryptions. **SubByteGen** AES implementation reveals the secret key in around 2000 encryptions.

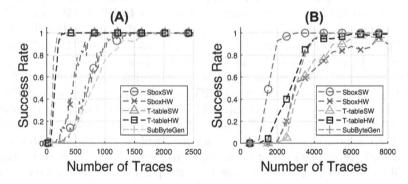

Fig. 4. (A) Power Analysis Attacks and (B) EM Attacks Against AES Implementations
on *SRISC*-SASEBO.

The EM attack results for identical AES implementations are presented in
Fig. 4-(B). **SboxSW** AES implementation required 3000 encryptions to reveal

the secret key. **T-tableHW** and **SubByteGen** AES implementations reveal the secret key in around 6000 encryptions. **SboxHW** and **T-tableSW** AES implementations require around 8000 encryptions to reveal the secret key.

The power analysis attacks were carried out on **BalSboxSW** AES implementation which uses a balanced Sbox lookup table stored in the software, and the CPA attack success rates are shown in the Fig. 5a –success rates for each key byte (K0 to K15) of the secret key is shown. Fourteen bytes (of 16 bytes) of the secret key were revealed in around 18,000 encryptions.

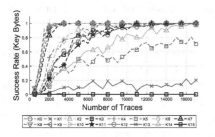 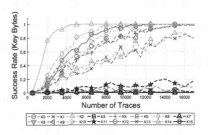

(a) **BalSboxSW** AES Implementation   (b) **BalSboxHW** AES implementation

Fig. 5. Power Analysis Attacks on Balanced AES Implementations.

The power analysis attack results on the **BalSboxSW** AES implementation are shown in Fig. 5b –success rates for each key byte (K0 to K15) of the secret key are shown. Eight bytes of the secret key were revealed in around 18,000 encryptions. The 18,000 encryption limit is due to the 16GB memory limit of the NVIDIA Tesla P100 GPU which is used to perform CPA attacks.

The cache timing attack vulnerabilities were tested for **SboxSW** and **T-tableSW** AES implementations using hardware counters explained in the Sect. 4.3. The cycle count for first 50 encryptions are shown in the Fig. 6-(A) for **SboxSW** AES implementation and in the Fig. 6-(B) for **T-tableSW** AES implementation. According to the Fig. 6-(A), the first encryption results in cache misses. Once the caches are filled with precalculated lookup table entries, the number of clock cycles remains constant at 29,164, irrespective of the plaintext.

According to the Fig. 6-(B), **T-tableSW** AES implementation shows a higher variation in elapsed clock cycles in the first 4–6 encryptions. Once the caches are filled, the number of clock cycles remains constant at 2,554, irrespective of the plaintext. We believe that by resetting the RISC-V core, reducing cache sizes or flushing the caches, more sophisticated cache timing attacks can be mounted.

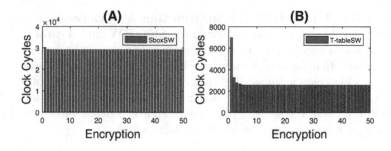

Fig. 6. Elapsed Time on *SRISC*-SASEBO for (A)–**SboxSW** and (B)–**T-tableSW**.

The resource utilisation of *SRISC*-SASEBO on a Xilinx Kintex-7 325T FPGA is calculated using Xilinx Vivado 2015.4 and tabulated in Table 1. The first column of the Table 1 depicts the resource category of the FPGA. The second column shows the name of the resource, such as lookup tables (LUT), FlipFlops (FF), BlockRAMs (BRAM), etc. The third and fourth columns depict the resource utilisation of *SRISC* and the number of resources available in the Xilinx Kintex-7 FPGA, respectively. The resource utilisation percentage is shown in the fifth column. According to Table 1, *SRISC* implementation on SASEBO GIII consumes around 22% LUTs, 6% of FFs and 16% of BRAMs and 10% MMCM.

Table 1. Resource Utilisation of *SRISC*-SASEBO on Xilinx Kintex-7 325T FPGA.

	Resource	Utilisation	Available	Utilisation %
Logic	LUT	46,599	203,800	22.87
	DSP	24	840	2.86
Memory	LUTRAM	2,422	64,000	3.78
	FF	26,603	407,600	6.53
	BRAM	73.5	445	16.52
Connections	IO	119	400	29.75
Clock	BUFG	5	32	15.63
	MMCM	1	10	10.0

8 Discussion

In this paper, we used a SASEBO GIII board equipped with a Xilinx Kintex-7 325T FPGA to demonstrate *SRISC* soft processor SCA attack framework. The Bitstreams for other variants of SASEBO GIII (with Kintex-7 70T and 160T FPGAs) can be directly compiled by modifying the FPGA part number. Based on the number of resources available on each FPGA, 94% and 38% of LUT utilisation is shown for a SASEBO GIII board equipped with a Xilinx Kintex-7 70T or a Kintex-7 160T FPGA, respectively.

The information leakage of Sbox table lookups in both software and hardware implementations are smaller than that of T-table lookups. Even though the information leakage of **SboxHW** is significant when compared to **SboxSW** (according to the Fig. 4-(A)), **BalSboxHW** AES implementation leaks less information via power dissipation (according to the Fig. 5b) compared to **BalSboxSW**. This shows the advantages of hybrid countermeasures which use both hardware and software components to achieve power analysis attack resistance.

9   Conclusion

This paper presents an open-source SCA attack framework using RISC-V soft processor system to test power, EM and timing attack vulnerabilities. The power and EM analysis attack results are presented for five AES implementations. Cache timing attack vulnerabilities are presented. The hardware/software co-design-based countermeasure implemented on *SRISC* showed reduced information leakage compared to an identical software implementation.

References

1. SRISC github repository. (2023). https://github.com/dnjayasinghe/SRISC
2. Agrawal, D., Archambeault, B., Rao, J.R., Rohatgi, P.: The EM side—channel(s). In: Kaliski, B.S., Koç, K., Paar, C. (eds.) CHES 2002. LNCS, vol. 2523, pp. 29–45. Springer, Heidelberg (2003). https://doi.org/10.1007/3-540-36400-5_4
3. Arora, A., Ambrose, J.A., Peddersen, J., Parameswaran, S.: A double-width algorithmic balancing to prevent power analysis side channel attacks in AES. In: ISVLSI 2013, pp. 76–83 (2013). https://doi.org/10.1109/ISVLSI.2013.6654626
4. Asanović., et al.: The rocket chip generator. Tech. Rep. UCB/EECS-2016-17, EECS Department, University of California, Berkeley (2016). http://www2.eecs.berkeley.edu/Pubs/TechRpts/2016/EECS-2016-17.html
5. Barthe, L., Benoit, P., Torres, L.: Investigation of a masking countermeasure against side-channel attacks for RISC-based processor architectures. In: FPL 2010, pp. 139–144 (2010)
6. Bernstein, D.J.: Cache-timing attacks on AES. Tech. rep. (2005)
7. Brier, E., Clavier, C., Olivier, F.: Correlation power analysis with a leakage model. In: Joye, M., Quisquater, J.J. (eds.) CHES 2004, vol. 3156, pp. 16–29 (2004)
8. of California Berkeley, U.: How can i parameterize my rocket chip (2019). https://github.com/chipsalliance/rocket-chip#-how-can-i-parameterize-my-rocket-chip
9. Canright, D.: A very compact S-Box for AES. In: Rao, J.R., Sunar, B. (eds.) CHES 2005. LNCS, vol. 3659, pp. 441–455. Springer, Heidelberg (2005). https://doi.org/10.1007/11545262_32
10. De Cherisey, E., Guilley, S., Rioul, O., Jayasinghe, D.: Template attacks with partial profiles and Dirichlet priors: application to timing attacks. HASP 2016 (2016). https://doi.org/10.1145/2948618.2948625
11. De Mulder, E., Gummalla, S., Hutter, M.: Protecting RISC-V against side-channel attacks, pp. 45:1–45:4. DAC 2019 (2019)

12. De Mulder, E., Gummalla, S., Hutter, M.: How to protect RISC-V against side-channel attacks? (2018). https://content.riscv.org/wp-content/uploads/2018/12/How-to-protect-RISC-V-Side-Channel-Attack-Elke-Samatha-and-Michael.pdf
13. EMEA, R.G.S.: Designing a custom AXI-lite slave peripheral (2014). https://cas.tudelft.nl/Education/courses/et4351/SILICA_Xilinx_Designing_a_custom_axi_slave_rev1.pdf
14. Foundation, R.V.: RISC-V cores (2019). https://riscv.org/risc-v-cores
15. Gaspar, L., Fischer, V., Bossuet, L., Fouquet, R.: Secure extension of FPGA general purpose processors for symmetric key cryptography with partial reconfiguration capabilities. ACM Trans. Reconfigurable Technol. Syst. 5(3), 16:1–16:13 (2012). https://doi.org/10.1145/2362374.2362380
16. Groß, H., Jelinek, M., Mangard, S., Unterluggauer, T., Werner, M.: Concealing secrets in embedded processors designs. In: CARDIS 2016, pp. 89–104 (2016)
17. Jayasinghe, D., Ragel, R., Ambrose, J., Ignjatovic, A., Parameswaran, S.: Advanced modes in AES: are they safe from power analysis based side channel attacks? In: ICCD 2014, pp. 173–180 (2014). https://doi.org/10.1109/ICCD.2014.6974678
18. Karri, R., Wu, K., Mishra, P., Kim, Y.: Fault-based side-channel cryptanalysis tolerant Rijndael symmetric block cipher architecture. In: DFT 2001, pp. 427–435 (2001)
19. Kocher, P.C.: Timing attacks on implementations of Diffie-Hellman, RSA, DSS, and other systems. In: Koblitz, N. (ed.) CRYPTO 1996. LNCS, vol. 1109, pp. 104–113. Springer, Heidelberg (1996). https://doi.org/10.1007/3-540-68697-5_9
20. Kocher, P.C., Jaffe, J., Jun, B.: Differential power analysis, pp. 388–397. CRYPTO 1999 (1999)
21. Lab./UEC, S.: Sakura-x (2019). http://satoh.cs.uec.ac.jp/SAKURA/hardware/SAKURA-X.html
22. LowRISC: Lowrisc version 0.2 overview (2015). https://www.lowrisc.org/docs/untether-v0.2/overview/
23. lowRISC: BBL: Berkeley boot loader (2019). https://www.lowrisc.org/docs/build-berkeley-boot-loader/
24. Mane, S., Taha, M., Schaumont, P.: Efficient and side-channel-secure block cipher implementation with custom instructions on FPGA. In: FPL 2012, pp. 20–25 (2012)
25. Mangard, S., Oswald, E., Popp, T.: Power Analysis Attacks. Springer, Boston, MA (2007). https://doi.org/10.1007/978-0-387-38162-6
26. Muhammad Arsath, C.R.: A framework for evaluation of side-channel leakage in a RISC-V processor (2018). https://content.riscv.org/wp-content/uploads/2018/07/1000-19.07.18-Muhammad-Arsath-Chester-Rebeiro-IIT-Madras.pdf
27. Tillich, S., Kirschbaum, M., Szekely, A.: SCA-resistant embedded processors: The next generation, pp. 211–220. ACSAC 2010 (2010)
28. Tiri, K., Verbauwhede, I.: A digital design flow for secure integrated circuits. Trans. Comp.-Aided Des. Integ. Cir. Sys. 25(7), 1197–1208 (2006)
29. Weiß, M., Heinz, B., Stumpf, F.: A Cache Timing Attack on AES in Virtualization Environments, pp. 314–328 (2012)
30. Xilinx: Cost-optimized portfolio product tables and product selection guide 2015. https://www.xilinx.com/support/documentation/selection-guides/ultrascale-plus-fpga-product-selection-guide.pdf
31. Xilinx: AXI interconnect PG059 (2017). https://www.xilinx.com/support/documentation/ip_documentation/axi_interconnect/v2_1/pg059-axi-interconnect.pdf

From Opacity to Clarity: Leveraging XAI for Robust Network Traffic Classification

Chamara Sandeepa[1]([✉]), Thulitha Senevirathna[1], Bartlomiej Siniarski[1],
Manh-Dung Nguyen[2], Vinh-Hoa La[2], Shen Wang[1], and Madhusanka Liyanage[1]

[1] School of Computer Science, University College Dublin, Dublin, Ireland
{abeysinghe.sandeepa,thulitha.senevirathna}@ucdconnect.ie,
{bartlomiej.siniarski,shen.wang,madhusanka}@ucd.ie
[2] Montimage EURL, Paris, France
{manhdung.nguyen,vinh_hoa.la}@montimage.com

Abstract. A wide adoption of Artificial Intelligence (AI) can be observed in recent years over networking to provide zero-touch, full autonomy of services towards the next generation Beyond 5G (B5G)/6G. However, AI-driven attacks on these services are a major concern in reaching the full potential of this future vision. Identifying how resilient the AI models are against attacks is an important aspect that should be carefully evaluated before adopting these services that could impact the privacy and security of billions of people. Therefore, we intend to evaluate resilience on Machine Learning (ML)-based use case of network traffic classification and attacks on it during model training and testing stages. For this, we use multiple resilience metrics. Furthermore, we investigate a novel approach using Explainable AI (XAI) to detect network classification-related attacks. Our experiments indicate that attacks can clearly affect the model integrity, which is measurable with the metrics and detectable with XAI.

Keywords: AI Resilience · Explainable AI · AI Attacks · Activity Classification · Communication Networks

1 Introduction

Real-world use of AI can have various caveats. Once deployed in the cloud, the models will constantly undergo different types of intrusion attempts. Although pragmatically, these attempts are unlikely to pass through the API gateway; it is not a certainty that it will be the case always. On the off chance that one of these attacks becomes successful, the model can be either stolen, taken under the control of the attacker, or completely/partially disabled. Therefore, achieving model robustness requires constant analysis of the model for various attacks.

However, despite the efforts to implement security and privacy, ML can still undergo numerous attacks that can compromise trust in the final outcome of the model. These attacks include evasion, poisoning, backdoor, and inference attacks [6]. This can create an issue in applying AI to real-world applications such as network automation. If an AI model performing critical network operations is compromised, the user's data that is handled via the AI is at risk, and the end users can lose trust in the network [13]. Yet, AI-driven automation is expected to be the future, which requires fully automated solutions to handle complex networks with trillions of devices in beyond 5G.

Hence, analysing a model's resilience against attacks is essential in AI before integrating it into a real-world application in future networks. A major component in resilience analysis is the metrics used to analyse the models. These metrics can uncover information regarding the model and its effectiveness against attacks. However, these metrics need to be customized during the implementation process for each attack type. By identifying the vulnerabilities and the model's effectiveness against attacks, stakeholders can make important decisions regarding the model and the system's health. To further verify and obtain more detailed information, the stakeholders can be provided with explanations generated with XAI methods. XAI is a set of mechanisms that can reveal the information on the black-box AI models, explaining how the AI decision-making process is done [15]. In this paper, we investigate on the possibility of using XAI as a detection tool for resilience attacks against AI by observing changes in post-hoc explanations with the attacks.

As a practical scenario of using AI in networking, we use a target use case of network activity classification, which can be regarded as an essential component in future network automation processes. It can differentiate various types of data transmitted over the network, which can be used for tasks such as scaling and prioritising highly demanding traffic, identifying malicious traffic, and personalisation services. To analyse the resilience of the network activity classifier, we launch two attacks: poisoning and evasion attacks. Then, we analyse the metrics and use XAI to determine if it is possible to identify attack scenarios.

1.1 Our Contributions

Despite many techniques to implement ML-based systems on networks, we observe a lack of metrics for resilience evaluation in the related literature. Moreover, the analysis of the impact of attacks on AI models via XAI is a novel area that can be considered as a potential path for attack detection. We bring the discussion of these topics, which are essential aspects to be considered for future network-based AI. Therefore, we summarise **our contributions** as follows:

- Presenting a use case of network activity classification model and launching network attacks against the resilience of the model.
- Assessing two attacks, evasion, and poisoning of ML models via multiple metrics, including measuring the impact on the models and complexity of the attacks.
- Performing a comprehensive XAI Shapley Additive Explanations (SHAP)-based attack analysis on the two attacks under different conditions.

We also provide an open-source repository[1] that consists of the implementation of this work, along with the dataset sources.

The rest of the sections are arranged as follows. Section 2 discusses associated works in the AI-based network classification use case and possible attacks. Details of our system model are presented in Sect. 3. Section 4 provides methods for implementing AI attacks on the system model. Section 5 provides experiments and their results. We discuss possible research directions in Sect. 6. The paper is summarised and concluded in Sect. 7.

2   Related Works

AI-based network traffic analysis is an important aspect that network systems should maintain for maintaining a secure and efficient network environment. Several works are available in the literature that has implemented AI-based systems to analyse network traffic. Authors in [7] present a detection technique for slowDoS attacks on encrypted traffic using clustering-based AI. Work in [1] uses Neural Networks (NN) and Principal Component Analysis (PCA) to analyse and classify network traffic for potential identification of malware traffic. In [2], the authors develop a Recurrent Neural Network (RNN)-based heterogeneous traffic detection and classification system for 5G networks.

However, detecting vulnerabilities in such AI applications that classify the traffic is a significant concern since the models trained on AI also need to train on accurate data in a secure and private environment. For example, in decentralised systems such as distributed AI or Federated Learning (FL) [12], AI models are trained by aggregation of models trained by many clients. In such a case, providing guaranteed privacy and security for each client would not be feasible. Even centralised systems can be vulnerable to attacks, where attackers can exploit a vulnerability and alter the operations in the training of AI models.

Attacks such as data poisoning [3] can cause degradation in the performance of ML models. Here, an attacker attempts to cause damage to the model predictions by manipulating the input data used to train the model. Several types of poisoning attacks exist, which include: 1) untargeted poisoning, which hinders convergence of the target model, leading to denial-of-service, 2) targeted poisoning, which causes abnormal predictions for some inputs; and 3) backdoor attacks, that uses targeted poisoning attacks go unnoticed via techniques such as hidden triggers embedded in the training data [14]. In network traffic classification scenarios, an attacker may use this type of attack to evade attacker-specific malicious traffic by poisoning the model to be insensitive to malicious traffic.

Evasion attacks are another type of attack where the attacker aims to evade the decisions made by the learned model during the test time; however, unlike poisoning attacks, they do not interfere with the training data [4]. Instead, they add perturbations to the inference data, which can cause erroneous output from the trained model. If an evasion attack is made for tasks such as network traffic

---

[1] https://github.com/Montimage/activity-classification

classification scenarios, an attacker can successfully evade any malicious traffic by having a small perturbation, misleading the classification of the AI model, even if the model is trained accurately and safely in the training phase.

Therefore, by considering these issues, assessing the impact of these attacks on AI is a significant requirement to identify the level of resilience of the overall intelligent system against the attacks. Furthermore, having XAI-based inspection on the model outputs can provide more explainability on model behaviour. Especially with attacks, if the model behaviour is changed with attacks, XAI itself can be used as a potential detection mechanism against the attacks, even if the changes are subtle and not visible, merely observing model predictions. Thus, we have two benefits of using XAI in the use case: 1) enhancing model transparency via explanations and 2) its potential use to evaluate resilience against poisoning and evasion attacks. However, we observe a lack of related literature considering both these aspects of XAI. Hence, in our work, we highlight the novel concept of using XAI as a potential tool for network classification scenarios for the detection of adversarial attacks.

3   System Model

The network activity classification is based on users interacting with a user's end personal devices. An overview of the system model is presented in Fig. 1.

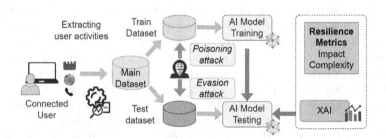

Fig. 1. Overview of the system with XAI and metrics implementation. The attacker is performing attacks; meanwhile, the resilience metrics and XAI analyse the impact, complexity, and possible detection of the attacks.

Here, network packets are analysed by a packet-capturing service. The metadata in the network packets includes the type of data that the payload of the packet consists of. This information is preprocessed and collected into a main dataset. Next, the data is split to train and test sets, where an AI model is first trained with the train data. The objective of this model is to classify the type of data that the payload consists of for a given metadata. Next, the trained model is tested with the test set to identify the performance of the model.

However, an attacker can interfere with the model training or the testing phase. They can launch poisoning attacks on the training data or target the test data to launch evasion attacks. Therefore, the model is vulnerable in both phases of the ML process.

Therefore, resilience metrics can be obtained to evaluate how the model is resilient against the attacks on AI. For this, we use two types of metrics: impact and complexity [11]. The impact metric measures how critical the attack is by analysing the changes in the accuracy metrics. The complexity is the level of difficulty of launching it from the attacker's side. Since we simulate the attacks, we can analyse the trade-off between the impact and complexity to get overall attack performance. Furthermore, we get the XAI metrics to identify internal changes in the ML model with the attacks. Such changes can lead to a potential attack detection technique, where we investigate from experiments in Sect. 5.

4 Attacks on AI

This section presents details of the two attacks we implement on the network traffic classification system. We use two attacks: 1) poisoning attacks during the training phase and 2) evasion attacks in the testing or inference phase. We highlight the procedure of launching the attacks, their variations, and constraints in the implementation.

4.1 Attacks at Training Time: Poisoning Attacks

The resilience of an explanatory platform can be evaluated by analysing how the platform would behave during an attack event. The observations would be the deviations in the model parameters when compared with the models before the attack and the output explanations provided by the trained models after the attack. The level of impact that an attack can be quantified with suitable metrics for the specific attack type. To simulate such a scenario, a poisoning attack was implemented on a network activity classification system, where an attacker is expected to perform different types of poisoning to the original dataset used to train the classification model. The overview of the attack is shown in Fig. 2.

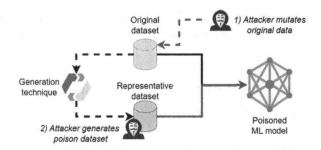

Fig. 2. Poisoning attacks on the activity classification model.

Here, the attacker can perform the data poisoning attack in two approaches: 1) modifying/mutating the original dataset or 2) adding new adversarial dataset examples to the existing dataset. For the second type, the attacker can use a generation technique like Generative Adversarial Networks (GAN) [16] for the attack. For the use case, we perform three types of poisoning attacks:

- **Random label flipping attack** - attacker randomly changes the labels in the original dataset. The objective of this attack is to reduce the utility of the model.
- **Targeted label poisoning attack** - a selected label type is favoured in flipping the labels by the attacker. The attacker intends to create an artificially biased dataset with the selected label to change the decision boundary of the model.
- **GAN-based poisoning attack** - here, the attacker uses a GAN to generate new data instances. Depending on the GAN-generated data's similarity level, this attack will be more challenging to detect. The main intention of the attacker here is to identify how the model's internals behave without disrupting its performance. Such poisoning can be used for privacy attacks like membership inference [17].

Metrics to Assess Poisoning Attack. For assessing how the model has changed with the attack, we use two metrics: impact and complexity.

The impact of the poisoning on the ML model can be defined as:

$$Impact = \frac{Error(F_p) - Error(F)}{Error(F)} \qquad (1)$$

where it measures the original accuracy of a benign ML model F compared to compromised model F_p. The impact is high when the difference between the benign and the compromised model is high.

The complexity metric is defined as:

$$Complexity = \frac{|D_p|}{|D + D_p|} \qquad (2)$$

which computes the ratio of poisoned data D_p and benign data D. It is regarded in poisoning that higher poisoning ratio results in higher complexity to perform the attack.

4.2   Attacks at Test Phase: Evasion Attacks

One of the popular attack types in adversarial AI is the evasion attack. Here the attacker attempts to misclassify the model output for maleficent advantages. In our implementation, we adopt FGSM (Fast Gradient Sign Method) [8] white box attack technique to generate adversarial data points used to test the web activity classification model. Here the intuition is to add a non-random noise with the direction same as the gradient of the cost function with respect to the data.

i.e., according to the authors of this attack, the direction of the perturbation only needs to have a positive dot product with the gradient of the cost function while the absolute magnitude of the perturbation is just enough to skip over the decision boundary. This evasion method can generate sequences of adversarial data points that can be generalized for ML models trained with different sub sets of training data. For the purpose of demonstrating the capability of metrics and XAI, FGSM attack is an ideal candidate because of the said extensibility with other ML models which we intend to expand the results.

Metrics to Assess Evasion Attacks. We use two resilience metrics, impact and complexity, that would manifest the attack's effectiveness against the models. The impact of evasion attacks is the attack success rate for a successfully evaded percentage of adversarial samples.

$$Impact = \frac{1}{|A|} \sum_{X_a \in A} \begin{cases} 1, & \text{if } F(X_a) \neq F(X) \\ 0, & \text{otherwise} \end{cases} \tag{3}$$

The complexity of the model can be defined as the CPU usage for the generation of evasion adversarial samples.

$$Complexity = \dot{t}_{cpu} \times N_{adv} \tag{4}$$

where t_{cpu} denotes the total CPU time and N_{adv} is the number of adversarial samples generated.

5 Experiments

This section is organised under each attack type we ran our experiments on. In addition to that, we also generate explanations through the XAI technique SHAP to provide a granular insight into the model features and their importance distribution.

5.1 Evaluating Poisoning Attacks

To perform the experiments, first, we trained a NN model for classifying the network testbed dataset. The data was collected from 279 training and 103 test instances of converted network PCAP files, with 22 features for each. We use a sequential model for the NN with 3 layers with 12, 8, and 3 dense layers, respectively. The configurations of the NN include Adam optimiser, batch size of 10, and binary cross-entropy for loss calculation. After training the model for 150 iterations, NN model test accuracy without attacks is obtained as 96.12%.

Impact and Complexity Analysis. Next, we perform poisoning attacks and assess the impact and complexity of the ML model over different poisoning types. As discussed, we have three types of poisoning: random swapping and poisoning by targeted flipping of labels were performed on the existing training data. The models are trained over varying poison percentages of 10%, 25%, 50%, and 100% of the original data being poisoned. We also generated a GAN-dataset using a small representative dataset from the original dataset, using a library called CTGAN². Then, we run GAN-based poisoning by mixing GAN data together with the original data. Next, the impact and complexity were calculated for each poisoning percentage. Graphs in Fig. 3 show how impact and complexity metrics vary over different poisoning levels.

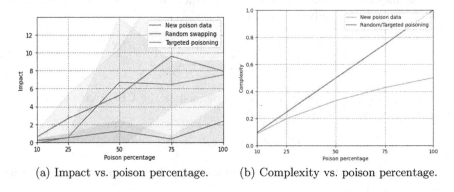

(a) Impact vs. poison percentage.   (b) Complexity vs. poison percentage.

Fig. 3. Impact and complexity metrics over different poison percentages.

Here, the impact of a new GAN-generated poisoning attack is relatively lower than the random and targeted poisoning since the new examples added by the GAN-generated dataset are very similar to the original data examples. In GAN-based poisoning, the attacker's main intention is not to reduce the model utility, since most GAN-based attacks are aimed for revealing privacy leakages without disrupting the model utility [17]. Therefore, the differences in original accuracy vs. the accuracy of the poisoned model here are lower. This results in lower impact. GAN-based attack is, therefore, more difficult to detect. However, for the other two attacks, the poisoned mode has significantly deviated from the original model, causing a higher impact. Similarly, the complexity metrics are higher for the random and targeted poisoning types than for the new GAN-generated poisoning.

XAI Feature Changes with Poisoning. To compare how key explanations from XAI are different with the poisoning attacks, SHAP [9] values are taken for the model for three scenarios of a) no poisoning, b) random label flipping, and c) new GAN-based poisoning as follows (Fig. 4):

---

² https://github.com/sdv-dev/CTGAN.

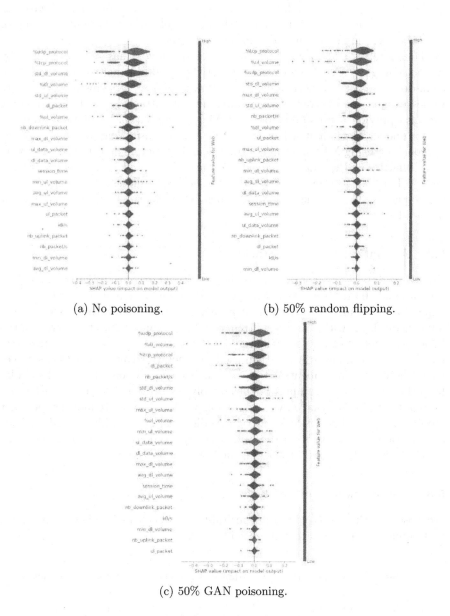

(a) No poisoning.

(b) 50% random flipping.

(c) 50% GAN poisoning.

Fig. 4. SHAP values variation over no poisoning vs. different poison types.

The SHAP values of the model without poisoning are similar to the GAN-based poisoning, which can be expected since they have a lesser impact on the model. However, in random flipping, the top feature values of the model have significant differences when compared with the model without poisoning, resulting from the high impact of the random flipping attack.

Therefore, in summary, the resilience of the model has been impacted by the poisoning attacks. They can be measured via suitable metrics for the attack scenario. For example, metrics such as distances among clustering of XAI feature values can be used to detect how impactful the attack is. Such XAI metrics can also provide a possibility of identifying a comparable deviation from the normal model when an attack event occurs. When considering the novelty of our approach by using XAI, poisoning attacks can initially be detected by observing the deviation of the most significant features compared with a non-poisoned model. This can further be analysed with the use of metrics that can quantify the impact of the attacks via XAI, which is considered a future work in our proposal.

5.2   Evaluating Evasion Attacks

The same dataset dimensions as in the poison attack (with 279 training data samples and 103 test samples) were also used in the evasion attack evaluation. A sequential keras model with 12 input nodes, 1 hidden layer with 8 nodes, and, a final output layer with 3 nodes is fitted with the training dataset. The rest of the hyper-parameters of the model were kept the same as the poisoning attack scenario. This neural network was then used to generate adversarial attack samples using the FGSM implementation in [10]. We generated 103 adversarial samples from the 103 test data samples we initially obtained. Exploiting the transferability of adversarial attacks [5], we expand our work on two more model types that are popularly used in network function predictions, namely, LightGBM(LGBM) and XGBoost. Here we used the same adversarial dataset generated using the neural network to launch attacks on the boosted tree models.

5.3   Observations and Analysis

We observed the following results in Table 1 for each metric before and after each model was exposed to the evasion attack.

Table 1. Attack performance for different attack types in multiple models.

Model	Attack type	Accuracy w/o attack	Accuracy with attack	Impact	Complexity
Neural Network	FSGM	96%	71%	29%	37.86 μs (1000 itr)
LGBM	Transferred from NN	94%	72%	28%	37.86 μs (1000 itr)
XGBoost	Transferred from NN	94%	54%	45%	37.86 μs (1000 itr)

Since the generation of adversarial samples was carried out with the neural networks, the model complexity is consistent with all the models. With the complexity metric, a stakeholder can realize the convenience for an adversary to generate these samples in various devices and compare different attack types on their expected frequency. This will allow system operators to efficiently manage defense mechanisms adhering to resource constraints.

We observed a significant drop in accuracy when evasion samples were involved. It is further manifested in the impact metric presenting how vulnerable the model is to FGSM attacks. For instance, the XGBoost model is 17% more likely to be affected by an adversarial model than a LightGBM model when compared to a LightGBM model with the same level of accuracy. This is valuable information for a stakeholder when deploying a model for real-world usage. To further strengthen our analysis, we also generate explanations that would be at the disposal of stakeholders, as shown in Fig. 5. It is apparent that the model's priorities, in terms of features, change in the face of adversarial attacks. The Shapley values for web activities have decreased (around 16%) for the *udp_protocol* causing the feature to drop to the second place in ranking while the importance of the *tcp_protocol* has almost doubled. Such a significant feature change would provide more meticulous information for stakeholders to take immediate action. Towards identifying evasion attacks on models, shapley value changes are also suitable as a validator alongside resilience metrics. However, with these revelations, in the future, it is possible to develop automated solutions with increased accuracy without losing accountability for detecting evasion attacks with high confidence.

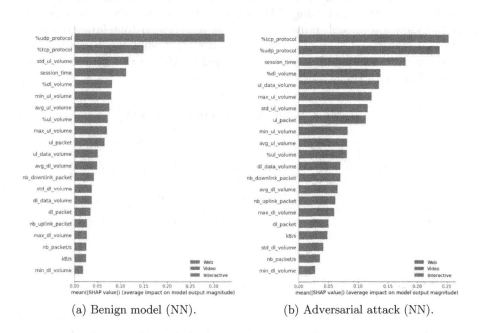

(a) Benign model (NN).   (b) Adversarial attack (NN).

Fig. 5. SHAP values for benign model vs. evasion attack event.

6   Discussion

The analysis of XAI in our work identifies that we can observe significant differences in a NN model undergoing an adversarial attack compared to a benign model. In evasion attacks, if the attacker starts flooding the model with evasion data points, the effects of the output will be reflected in the feature importance scores. This also depends on the frequency of the attackers' intrusions. In short, during the pre-deployment stage of a model, system developers can use the impact and complexity metrics to identify the vulnerability of the model against known evasion attacks, while XAI is more of a detection and reconciliation tool. In the case of poisoning attacks, the attack may go unrecognised in case if the attack is GAN-based. This also depends on the similarity of the produced GAN data with the original data of users. Obtaining such a representative sample from the original may also be difficult for an attacker unless they gain access to the original data or be an insider. Therefore, a GAN-produced poisoning attack may also be possible to detect and defend if we provide more security and privacy for the original data. Furthermore, the diversity and distribution of the original data can also affect the original reference model XAI outputs. For example, in the case of distributed ML like FL, many clients can have local models based on their non-Independent and Identically Distributed (non-IID) data that is specialised on a particular client. In such a case, XAI's outputs can vary from client to client. Detecting benign models from adversarial models via variations in XAI is a possibility to expand in the future.

Furthermore, when comparing the key outcomes of our work with the related works, we observe that none of the works related to network-based classifications discuss the potential of using XAI as a detection mechanism against attacks. A comparison of model resilience metrics of impact and complexity during an attack incident and their trade-offs is another key finding we delivered in our work that is not found in other works. Table 2 provides a summary comparison of our work with key highlights.

Table 2. Summary contribution of our work.

Characteristics	Ref [1]	Ref [3]	Ref [7]	Ref [16]	Ref [17]	Our work
Network related use case for B5G/6G AI and attack scenarios	✓	✓	✓	✓	✓	✓
Launching resilience attacks against trained ML models	✓	✓	–	✓	–	✓
Proposal of metrics to quantify resilience on the model during attacks	✓	✓	–	✓	–	✓
XAI-based visualisation and detection strategy	–	–	–	–	–	✓
Possible directions on enhancing resilience and limitations	–	–	✓	✓	✓	✓

7   Conclusion

In this research, we analysed resilience metrics of impact and complexity of two adversarial attacks, poisoning and evasion attacks, against network activity classification scenarios. We observe that the impact and complexity can vary in different attack categories, which makes attacks such as GAN-based poisoning relatively difficult to detect, meanwhile having less complexity on the attacker's side. Thus, attacks that cause a lesser impact on the model can be more threatening to the security and privacy of the model due to its difficulty in tracing the attack. The XAI analysis with SHAP also shows that the higher the attack's impact on the model, the easier it is to determine by observing the variation of the SHAP-based feature contributions. We observe higher variation over the adversarial attacks, which cause a higher impact on the model. Therefore, XAI can be applied as a potential detection mechanism for attack detection. It can easily be adapted for assessing the model's possible resilience compromises before deploying the AI models in real-world network applications.

Acknowledgment. This work is partly supported by European Union in SPATIAL (Grant No: 101021808), and Science Foundation Ireland under CONNECT phase 2 (Grant no. 13/RC/2077_P2) projects.

References

1. Arivudainambi, D., KA, V.K., Visu, P., et al.: Malware traffic classification using principal component analysis and artificial neural network for extreme surveillance. Comput. Commun. **147**, 50–57 (2019)
2. Artem, V., Ateya, A.A., Muthanna, A., Koucheryavy, A.: Novel AI-based scheme for traffic detection and recognition in 5G based networks. In: Galinina, O., Andreev, S., Balandin, S., Koucheryavy, Y. (eds.) NEW2AN/ruSMART -2019. LNCS, vol. 11660, pp. 243–255. Springer, Cham (2019). https://doi.org/10.1007/978-3-030-30859-9_21
3. Aryal, K., Gupta, M., Abdelsalam, M.: Analysis of label-flip poisoning attack on machine learning based malware detector. In: 2022 IEEE International Conference on Big Data (Big Data), pp. 4236–4245. IEEE (2022)
4. Deldjoo, Y., Noia, T.D., Merra, F.A.: A survey on adversarial recommender systems: from attack/defense strategies to generative adversarial networks. ACM Comput. Surv. (CSUR) **54**(2), 1–38 (2021)
5. Demontis, A., et al.: Why do adversarial attacks transfer? Explaining transferability of evasion and poisoning attacks. In: 28th USENIX Security Symposium (USENIX Security 19), pp. 321–338 (2019)
6. Eigner, O., et al.: Towards resilient artificial intelligence: survey and research issues. In: 2021 IEEE International Conference on Cyber Security and Resilience (CSR), pp. 536–542. IEEE (2021)
7. Garcia, N., Alcaniz, T., González-Vidal, A., Bernabe, J.B., Rivera, D., Skarmeta, A.: Distributed real-time SlowDoS attacks detection over encrypted traffic using artificial intelligence. J. Netw. Comput. Appl. (2021)
8. Goodfellow, I.J., Shlens, J., Szegedy, C.: Explaining and harnessing adversarial examples. arXiv preprint arXiv:1412.6572 (2014)
9. Lundberg, S.M., Lee, S.I.: A unified approach to interpreting model predictions. In: Advances in Neural Information Processing Systems (2017)
10. Nicolae, M.I., et al.: Adversarial robustness toolbox v1.2.0. CoRR 1807.01069 (2018). https://arxiv.org/pdf/1807.01069

11. Park, S., et al.: Deliverable 2.2 define parameters and elements to construct accountability, resilience, and privacy metrics. European Union, Horizon 2020 SPATIAL (2023)
12. Pei, J., Zhong, K., Jan, M.A., Li, J.: Personalized federated learning framework for network traffic anomaly detection. Comput. Netw. **209**, 108906 (2022)
13. Sandeepa, C., Siniarski, B., Kourtellis, N., Wang, S., Liyanage, M.: A survey on privacy for B5G/6G: new privacy challenges, and research directions. J. Ind. Inf. Integr., 100405 (2022)
14. Tian, Z., Cui, L., Liang, J., Yu, S.: A comprehensive survey on poisoning attacks and countermeasures in machine learning. ACM Comput. Surv. (2022)
15. Xu, F., Uszkoreit, H., Du, Y., Fan, W., Zhao, D., Zhu, J.: Explainable AI: a brief survey on history, research areas, approaches and challenges. In: Tang, J., Kan, M.-Y., Zhao, D., Li, S., Zan, H. (eds.) NLPCC 2019. LNCS (LNAI), vol. 11839, pp. 563–574. Springer, Cham (2019). https://doi.org/10.1007/978-3-030-32236-6_51
16. Zhang, J., Chen, J., Wu, D., Chen, B., Yu, S.: Poisoning attack in federated learning using generative adversarial nets. In: 2019 18th IEEE International Conference on Trust, Security and Privacy In Computing and Communications/13th IEEE International Conference on Big Data Science and Engineering (TrustCom/BigDataSE), pp. 374–380. IEEE (2019)
17. Zhang, J., Zhang, J., Chen, J., Yu, S.: GAN enhanced membership inference: a passive local attack in federated learning. In: ICC 2020–2020 IEEE International Conference on Communications (ICC), pp. 1–6. IEEE (2020)

Author Index

D. Herath et al. (Eds.): APANConf 2023, CCIS 1995, p. 139, 2024.
https://doi.org/10.1007/978-3-031-51135-6

Printed in the United States
by Baker & Taylor Publisher Services